SPECIAL TIMES FOR PARENTS & KIDS TOGETHER

Lisa Lyons Durkin

Together Activities
and Additional
Material by
Kathy Faggella

Art by Debby Dixler

WARNER BOOKS

A Warner Communications Company

The following pages are reprinted from Crayons, Crafts and Concepts by Kathy Faggella by permission of First Teacher, Inc.: 38,45,46,47,49,50,51,52,56,93,100,104, and 106.

The following pages are reprinted from Concept Cookery by Kathy Faggella by permission of First Teacher, Inc.: 37,40,47,48,50, and 96.

The following pages are reprinted from Celebrate Every Day by permission of First Teacher, Inc.: 24,27,29,34,35,36,43,48,53,63,65,72,79,81, and 91.

Warner Books, Inc., 666 Fifth Avenue, New York, NY 10103

A Warner Communications Company

Design by Alice Cooke, A to Z Design, NYC

Cover Design by Alice Cooke; Illustration by Debby Dixler

Copyediting and skills charts by Martha A. Hayes

Editorial Assistant: Kathleen M. Hyson

Layout and Typesetting: Michael R. Durkin

Technical Advisor: Jim Faggella

Printed in the United States of America
First Printing: November 1987
10 9 8 7 6 5 4 3 2 1

Library of Congress Cataloging-in-Publication Data

Durkin, Lisa Lyons.
    Special times for parents and kids together.

    1. Amusements. 2. Games. 3. Creative activties
and seat work. 4. Outdoor recreation for children.
I. Title.
GV1203.D87 1987   649'.5   87-23124
ISBN 0-446-38680-4 (pbk.) (U.S.A.)
    0-446-38681-2 (pbk.) (Canada)

ACKNOWLEDGMENTS

I would like to thank the "parents and kids" who inspired my research: the Abrams, Currys, DeMarias, Dixlers, Garratts, Johnson-Kerners, Mayers, and many others.

I would also like to gratefully acknowledge the contributions of everyone who has written articles for First Teacher over the past eight years. And, I wish to acknowledge the specific articles in First Teacher from which I researched the ideas for Special Times for Parents and Kids Together.

Chapter 1: "A Special Time for Me" by Jean Stangl (June, 1984);"Brainstorming" by Janet Horowitz (October, 1985); "Building Trust" by June Gould (January, 1980);"Building Your Child's Self-Esteem" by Saf Lerman (September 1986);"Choices,Choices" Mary Beth Spann (September, 1986);"Discipline with Love" by Beverly R. Thurman (September, 1986);"Getting There Kid-style" by Sandra Gratias (June, 1983);"Guide the Way" by Dr. Nancy Reckinger (October, 1985);"Guiding Behavior" by Gene Rotas (January, 1980);"How Do We View Growth and Change in the Young Child?" by Nancy McKeever (February, 1980);"I'm Ok--You're OK" by Dr. Nancy Reckinger (September, 1986);"Lots of 'Worlds' to Explore" by Bernard Ryan, Jr. (June, 1981);"Mementos from School" by Dr. Sally Bing (June, 1986);"Open the Door" by Sherry Burrell (October, 1985);"Peak Experiences" by Dr. Nancy Reckinger (June, 1986);"Positive Comments Count" by Sherry Bahnsen (September, 1986);"The Greatest Treasures" by Martha A. Hayes (June, 1986);"The Total Child" by Nancy McKeever (January,1980)

Chapter 2: "A Photo Safari" by Francine Jaroncyzk (June, 1984);"Bikes and Trikes" by Karel Kilimnik (July/August, 1986);"Blow Up Some Fun" by Dr. Margery A. Kranyik (March, 1985);"Cloudy Days" by Janet Horowitz (March, 1985);"Going to the Zoo" by Sherry Burrell (July/August, 1986);"Learning with the Penguins" by Peter Feldner and Georgia Wright (June, 1984);"One Man's Opinion" by David L. Giveans (June, 1981);"Scribbles, Seurat, and Sculpture" by Janet Horowitz (June, 1986);"The Moon and Beyond" by Jeannine Perez (March, 1985);"Trekking with Tots" by Maria and Jeremy Michele (July/August, 1986);"Visit a Learning Farm" by Martha A. Hayes (July/August, 1986);"Where's the Wind" by Jean Stangl (March, 1985);"Who Lives in the Meadow?" by Dr. Margery A. Kranyik (June, 1984)

Chapter 3: "Begin with an Ending" by Dr. Lydia A. Duggins (June, 1984);"Bubbles and Rainbows" by Dr. Carole Cox (April, 1987);"Busy Kids: Happy Parents" by Janet Horowitz (June, 1984);"Day Camping" by Dr. Margery A. Kranyik (June, 1983);"Playing Alone" by Dr. Margery A. Kranyik (May, 1987);"Save the Summer" by Mary Beth Spann (July/August 1986);"Summer Fun Outdoors" by Susan Coons (June 1984);"Summer Magic" by Joanne Bell (June, 1984)

Chapter 4: "All Aboard" by Denise Moore Nelson (July/August, 1986);"By the Sea, By the Sea" by Dr. Margery A. Kranyik (July, 1983);"Getting There 'Kid-style'" by Sandra Gratias (June 1983);"In the Book Corner" by Martha A. Hayes (July/August 1986);"Pack Up your Routines" by Dr. Billie Joan Thomas (June, 1983);"Preparing Children for Trips" by Dr. Sally Bing (June, 1984);"Special Travel Plans" by Harriet Miller Ettenson (June, 1983);"Taking Off" by Sandra Gratias (July/August 1986);"The FTP Camping Guide" by Janet Horowitz (June, 1981);"Traveling with Kids" by Harriet Miller Ettenson (June, 1981);"Trip Tips" by Ellen Hasbrouck (June, 1983)

Chapter 5: "Celebrate the Season" by Jeannine Perez (December, 1985);"Choosing Toys for the Young Child" by Janet Horowitz (November, 1982);"Creative Ways to Make the Preholiday Period Pass Quickly" by Sandra Gratias (December, 1985);"Holidays at Home" by Saf Lerman (December, 1985);"Make Holidays and Parties Real Celebrations for Pre-schoolers" by Nancy McKeever (October 1980);"Not from the Toy Store" by Kathleen Koons (December, 1985);"Open Feelings" by Dr. Nancy Reckinger (February, 1985);"Photos for Fun" by Janet Horowitz (December, 1985);"Resources for the Holidays" by Anne H. Leone (December, 1985);"Valentine's Day Favorites" by Francine Jaronczyk (February, 1987)

Chapter 6: "In the Book Corner" by Dr. Anne H. Leone (October, 1983);"Leave the Cupcakes at Home" by Janet Horowitz (October, 1983);"Let's Have a Party" by Dr. Lydia A. Duggins (October, 1983);"New Birthday Ideas" by Mary Beth Spann (October, 1983);"Teddy Bear Tea" by Mary Beth Spann (October, 1983)

Chapter 7: "When a Child Is Sick...How to Tell What to Do" by Janet Horowitz (June, 1980);"Being the Baby Is Never Easy" by Harriet Miller Ettenson (February 1982);"Big Questions About Life" by Dr. Nancy Reckinger (May 1985);"Bringing Problems Home From School" by Saf Lerman (February 1986);"Changing Schools" by Dr. Sally Bing (July/August 1986);"Coping with Divorce" by Dr. Margery A. Kranyik (May 1985);"Do You Set an Example When You Are Sick?" by Fretta Reitzes (June, 1980);"First, Second, Third...at Home" by Gene Rotas (September 1980);"Fives in Need" by Bernard Ryan, Jr. (February 1982);"Helping More by Helping Less" by Sherry Burrell (September 1980);"Help Kids Cope" by Dr. Lydia A. Duggins (February 1982);"Home Grown Problems" by Sherry Burrell (February 1986);"In the Book Corner" by Dr. Anne H. Leone (May 1985);"Kids Are Creative Copers" by Sandra Edwards (February 1982);"Make a 'Quiet-Time' Toy Bag" by Janet Horowitz (June, 1980);"Moving Away" by Jean Stangl (July/August 1986);"Papers and Paintings" by Mary Beth Spann (June 1986);"Phyllis Halloran's Book Corner" by Phyllis Halloran (February 1982);"RX Parents of a Sick Child" by Janet Horowitz (June, 1980);"Security Blankets" by Dr. Lydia A. Duggins (February, 1985);"Signs of Health" by Ellen Goldstein (April, 1985);"Single Parenting" by Gene Rotas (June, 1981);"Taking the Sting Out of 'Good-bye'" by Nancy McKeever (Preview Issue);"Teacher to Parent" by Jeannine Perez (July/August 1986);"What a Way to Cope" by Nancy McKeever (February 1982);"When a Child Is Sick" by Janet Horowitz (June, 1980);"Whose Fault Is It?" by Harriet Miller Ettenson (July 1982)

My special thanks to Dr. Ruth Mayer for her insights and editorial comments on Chapter 7.

TABLE OF

CONTENTS

ACTIVITIES AND RECIPES TO DO TOGETHER

A book is like a child — it needs nurturing to reach its potential. And so, with affection and appreciation, I dedicate *Special Times For Parents And Kids Together* to Martha Hayes, Kathy Hyson, and Mike Durkin who played such an important role in its growth and development.

Foreword

This book is full of many happy memories for me. The memories come from the special times I have shared with my four-year-old daughter, my stepsons, and all of their friends and parents. These are many of the special times that I will share with you in the pages that follow.

All of the activities, projects, recipes, and ideas for excursions in this book come from my own experiences and from the insights I have gained from my work as editor of First Teacher, a monthly newspaper written for and by Early Childhood educators. Like many of you, I am a busy working parent, who has a limited amount of "special time" to spend with my young child, so I cherish the weekends, holidays, and vacations I can share with my family. Luckily, my work brings me in contact with thousands of easy, practical, classroom-tested ideas that I can modify to fit these special times—ideas that help me stimulate and guide my child.

From my work, I have learned one basic fact of child development of which I feel every parent should be aware: a child does 80% of her lifetime learning in the first six years. Thus, we parents are truly "first teachers," providing those essential first learning experiences that enable our children to grow into happy, self-confident, productive individuals.

This may seem like a formidable task, especially since parents are not given a diploma in Early Childhood Education along with their child's birth certificate. But, actually, all parents have to do is to provide an environment where their child feels safe and confident to explore on her own. This is HOW young children learn.

WHAT do they learn? Every one of a child's early experiences is a learning experience, helping her grow physically, emotionally, intellectually, and socially. Young children learn everything—motor skills, like walking, climbing, drawing, cutting, and pasting; social skills, like sharing and waiting for a turn; concepts, like colors, opposites, and the seasons; language skills, like words, sentences, and later reading and writing; creativity—the list goes on and on. But, I feel that the most important lesson that we, "the first teachers," must teach our children before they start formal schooling is that they are special, capable, and lovable. At home, they must begin to develop a positive self-image.

And, that is the theme of this book. Here is a wealth of specific learning experiences, all adapted from activities used by teachers in Early Childhood classrooms, and presented in the context of the "special times" you spend with your child. But, more important, here is also a wealth of suggestions for helping your child develop self-discipline and self-esteem—ideas that can be woven into every part of family life.

The TOGETHER pages—art projects, recipes, games—are meant to introduce, follow up, or extend the other ideas in the book. Many of the projects can be used to absorb some of that youthful energy that comes from the anticipation of a special event. The activities are presented in visual, easy-to-read, sequential formats that hopefully will appeal to both you and your child.

The emphasis in all of these TOGETHER projects should be placed on the process, not the product. The fun and learning are in the doing, not the result. The more your child can do herself, the better. She will be learning to cut, paste, draw, mix, grate, peel—as well as many other fine motor skills. She will be practicing following directions and all of the basic thinking skills, which I discuss in depth in Chapter 1. AND, most of the projects are open-ended enough to encourage her creativity. None of the activities take a long time—30 minutes at the most—and most of the materials you need are easily found around the house. For me, these are two criteria for a successful project with a young child at home.

Not all of the TOGETHER projects will appeal to your child—or to you. Since the most valuable time you can spend with your child is that time when you are both relaxed and enjoying yourselves, it is important to choose those projects that will be fun for both of you. However, I do encourage you to try activities that your child is really excited about—even if they don't appear very challenging to you at first. Young enthusiasm is infectious; it can turn the most mundane experience into something really special.

This thought brings me to the real message of this book, Special Times for Parents and Kids Together. "Special times" mean more to me than weekends, holidays, vacations, and so on. They are different from the "quality time," which in my mind should be all of the time you spend with your child, whether you are sorting laundry together or reading a storybook

However "special times" have an almost magical quality to them. Last weekend, I was at the beach with my four-year-old daughter and I realized that sharing the experience was what made it special. I was able to tap into her innocent wonder and experience the sand, the waves, the seagulls, the whole scene in a fresh, exciting way. Her appreciation and sense of fun evoked wonderful memories of seaside adventures from my own childhood. Being at the beach with my four-year-old was a truly "special time" for me.

Similarly, my child's experience was special because she shared it with me. In my presence, she was able to tap her own ageless sense of curiosity. I gave her the sense of security which enabled her to reach out and make discoveries about the beach. Through my questions and my answers to her questions, we explored together. It was a really "special time" for both of us.

This book is about those potentially magical experiences that I call "special times." A trip to the zoo, an evening of star-gazing, a spooky Halloween, a day at the beach—all of these will take new meaning when you share them with a little one whom you love.

INTRODUCTION 1

Milestones

Choices

Guiding Behavior

Thinking Skills

Special Treasures

Planning Special Times

Milestones

Just as you should feel that all the time you spend with your child is quality time, you should not think of "special times" only as weekends, holidays, and vacations. There are so many special times in your child's preschool years—milestones of growth and development—that it would take a whole book just to list them. You could almost say that every day in your child's life is a holiday—a time for celebration.

When your child was an infant, it was easy to observe milestones—the first smile, each inch of growth, that first word, then crawling, climbing, and finally steps. The baby guidebooks told you what to expect and approximately when so you eagerly awaited each new accomplishment.

As your child gets older, however, these milestones become more difficult to observe and measure. Each child, for instance, has her own timetable for toilet-training, recognition of colors and shapes, and learning to share.

Yet, during this time of enormous intellectual, physical, emotional, and social growth, your child needs even more recognition and celebration of her development than she did as a baby. Your recognition of this growth and change nurtures your child's development and speeds it along. Just like adults, children grow and change when they feel good about themselves.

In fact, in my opinion, the most important thing you can help your child develop in preparation for school—and for her whole life—is GOOD SELF-ESTEEM. Your primary job is not to teach reading skills, not study aids, not basic concepts; it is, very simply, to give your child the feeling that she is able to do many things well, that she is capable and lovable.

Good self-esteem doesn't just happen to children. It grows like the body and develops like the mind. It grows as your child meets small challenges each day and gets positive feedback from you—even when she doesn't succeed.

So your most important teaching tools are a bagful of positive, constructive comments, tailored to fit each challenge your child undertakes. It doesn't have to be a new challenge—children like to repeat successes. It makes them feel secure and builds that all-important confidence they need to try something new. When you are asking your child questions, put a question about something unfamiliar between two questions that you know your child can answer with ease. In this way, you are building self-esteem at the same time as you are asking your child to meet a new challenge.

During those difficult times when you can't find many positive things to say about your child's present behavior, talk to her about her past milestones—accomplishments she may have forgotten. *"When you were just a year old, you walked for the first time. Daddy and I were so proud of you." "Do you remember when Grandma was sick last year? You made a picture for her. It made her feel much better."* These little boosts can be just the encouragement your child needs to try that new task.

Here are some tips that management consultants offer for making positive comments that really count in a business setting. Human nature being what it is, these tips can be applied to your child as well.

▶ First, be sure to make good eye contact with your child when you're offering a positive comment. It really gets across your sincerity. Also, with a "little listener," you'll be guaranteed that your message is heard.
▶ Next, be sure that you are close to your child when you speak to her. Again, this avoids any possible confusion about whom you are praising.
▶ Then, say what you feel. Tell your child exactly what she did that was so special and how you felt about it. Don't forget to tell her you love her for who she is, not just for what she does.

As well as speaking to your child about how special she is, make sure you take the time to listen closely to what she has to say. Self-confidence grows as children feel that the people they really care about are interested in their ideas, concerns, questions, and feelings.

AND, always remember: you can't make your child feel TOO good about herself. With all the new things she is experiencing in her early years, all the new people she is meeting, all the challenges she is facing every day, good self-esteem can make a tremendous difference in your child's development and happiness.

As a parent, you are in a position to structure your child's environment and activities to ensure positive experiences. Just as you childproof a toddler's room, you can "frustration-proof" your child's experiences by not introducing things before she is ready for them and certainly by not bringing them up in a succeed/fail situation.

To help your child grow and change, provide her with a rich environment that includes materials which can be used in many ways. In her preschool years, your child is an explorer. It is your job as "first teacher," to give her the experiences, situations, and materials that will allow her to make discoveries about the world and herself.

But, what is an environment that builds self-esteem and encourages exploration?

▶ It's a place that provides safety and encourages your child to take risks at the same time. Young children love repetition because it's safe and guarantees success, but in order to grow, they have to try new things and that means taking risks.
▶ It's a place that provides the security of reasonable limits.
▶ It's a place where mistakes are accepted as a natural part of the learning process.
▶ It's a place where CHOICES are allowed wherever possible.

Choices

THE "NO CHOICE"

The act of choosing options makes all of us, young children included, feel powerful and in control of our lives. This is particulary true for your preschooler, who has not had much say in her life up to this point. It's extremely important for her self-esteem and for her development on all levels that she learn to make decisions in situations where she has some control and to learn to accept those situations where there is no choice.

There are NO CHOICE situations where your child has absolutely no say in the decision-making process. These situations include all of those related to health and safety. *"You must wear a snowsuit and boots outside on a snowy day because if you don't, you may get sick." "You may not play with that knife because you could cut yourself."*

There are many times when your child will have no choice about coming or going. *"We have to stay home this weekend."* This is non-negotiable; but, you can soften the blow by adding, *"But, I want you to choose a game for the whole family to play on Saturday,"* or *"We will bake a cake together and you can choose the flavor."*

There are also times when you are just too rushed or feel too pressured to take time to discuss choices. Be firm and be sure to state a reason for your choice. *"I know you wanted to go to the zoo today, but we're going to the playground instead. I promised Billy's mom we would meet them there this morning."* Then, change the subject. It's pointless to go on and on with explanations and excuses when they won't change your decision. Your child should begin to realize that she can't have input into every situation.

Whenever you can't let your child participate in the decision-making process, be sure to explain the reasons why you decided what you did. This introduces your child to an important thinking skill—cause and effect. Often young children act and react without thinking about the results of their actions. It is so important that you help your child think about each result. Just saying, *"Because I said so."* may be a convenient excuse, but all you are really teaching your child is that "might makes right." She will sense the difference when you fail to give an understandable excuse.

Even when your child is a toddler, you can introduce her to the skill of decision-making by offering her LIMITED CHOICES—that is, choices from a limited number of possibilities. Often, you, as her first teacher, will have to guide your child in making the best choice. It may mean helping her try out various activities before she finds the one that is most enjoyable or the one that works best. Always try to get her to tell you why she made the choice she did. *"I'll go on the swing now because I want to feel like a bird flying."*

THE "LIMITED CHOICE"

Areas open to this type of negotiation include such possibilities as toys to play with, books to read, cereals to eat at breakfast, afternoon snacks, clothes to wear, even weekend excursions, rainy day projects, holiday decorations to make—when you set the limits. *"We can go to the zoo or on a picnic, but it is such a lovely day that we are going outside."* If you find your child taking forever to make up her mind about a decision, you can give her a gentle push. *"You may choose carrot sticks or raisins to put in the picnic basket, or I will choose one for you."*

Find as many opportunities as you can to give your child limited choices. Build up from simple either/or situations to choices between three or even four alternatives. Talk about the choices and help your child make decisions where necessary.

THE "UNLIMITED CHOICE"

Take care not to turn your life into one long game of "Let's Make a Deal." You don't want to hear all day long, *"I'll do this if you give me that..."* Don't hesitate to say, *"These are your choices. Choose one or I will have to choose for you."* or *"I'm sorry, but this time there is no choice."*

When your child is feeling comfortable with the idea of limited choices, you can introduce the concept of UNLIMITED CHOICE. This is not as free-wheeling as it sounds, and again, it provides practice in important thinking skills for your child. You can tell your child to choose any color blouse she wants to wear or draw anything on a blank piece of paper or pick up any leaves that have fallen to the ground in your yard without totally upsetting your household balance of power. Some children love to feel powerful through these unlimited choices; others may feel uncomfortable without some direction from you. Know your child and, if necessary, work up to this slowly.

There is one last choice-making situation which really helps develop your child's creative thinking skills, the FANTASY CHOICE. Here you pretend there is a choice where, in reality, none exists. For example, on a sunny, summer day, ask, *"What could we do if it was snowing out today?"* To make this choice, your child has to stretch her thinking into the realm of daydreams. Let your child act out her ideas, if possible. Sometimes, she may want to draw a picture to describe her fantasy choice. In fact, having a fantasy choice to make can take some of the disappointment out of a No Choice situation for your child. "What ifs" are terrific for car trips, waiting in line, and any time when you would like to occupy your child's mind with a little creative thinking.

THE "FANTASY" CHOICE

Guiding Behavior

"Special times" can become especially difficult times when your child is not behaving appropriately. Children learn to behave—in other words, self-discipline—through a trusting, loving relationship with an older person they care about. In fact, the word *discipline* comes from *disciple* which means "follower." Somehow over the years, discipline became confused with punishment; when it is, in reality, a process whereby a child learns what she should be doing. Punishment stresses what she should not do.

As your child's "first teacher," you are a guide helping your child develop self-discipline. To do this, first of all, it's a good idea to think about your goals for your child's behavior. For example, I want my child to be able to make good, clear decisions and, at the same time, always respect the feelings of other people. I want her to learn and continue to use behaviors that will allow her to develop her talents and abilities and become all she is capable of becoming.

Self-discipline develops slowly over the first five years of a person's life. When your child is a newborn, her needs are met by a loving adult. She knows someone will come when she cries. Through this trust, she develops the ability to wait a little while after her initial cry for help, secure in the knowledge that someone is coming. This is the first sign of self-discipline. When your child begins to move around, *"no"* becomes a word used by the people she trusts to keep her away from harmful situations. She learns the meaning of the word and tries hard to stop herself when she hears it. Hopefully, she also hears the words of encouragement and praise you use when she practices self control or needs a boost.

By the time she is three, your child has learned to stay away from many harmful situations, but, she still needs your guidance, encouragement, and praise. She needs to learn new behaviors for new experiences and relationships. She needs your help in making the "right" choices. Here again, you are your child's "first teacher." Just as there are many ways to teach basic concepts and skills, there are also different ways to guide your child's behavior.

Let me share some techniques used by Early Childhood teachers to help prevent troublesome behavior and, at the same time, positively reinforce behavior you want your child to learn.

▶ When you give directions to your child, use positive terms. Use *"do""* much more often than *"don't."*

▶ Give choices only when you mean to. (This takes a lot of thought sometimes!) Don't ask, *"Do you want to have lunch now?"* when what you really mean is, *"We're having lunch right this moment."*

▶ Be clear when you are guiding your child's behavior with words. *"It's time for bed"* may not be enough to get your child to brush her teeth, choose a book, and hop into bed.

▶ Use distraction to get your child to stop an inappropriate behavior.

▶ If distraction doesn't work, speak directly about the behavior. Say, *"If you interrupt all the time, I can't find out what your brother did at school today,"* instead of *" You're being a bad girl."* Don't make judgments when you are guiding your child's behavior. Always make sure she knows you love her and that she is a good person in your eyes.

Sometimes, actions speak louder than words.

▶ Give your child examples to follow—turn off the light when you are the last one to leave a room; be sure to say *"Please," "Thank you,"* and *"Excuse me"* when appropriate.

▶ Take your child by the hand and show her how to do things.

▶ When your child starts to act up, stand next to her. Your close presence will be a distraction in itself and it also lets her know you are in control.

▶ Remove your child from situations where she has lost control. Never be afraid to restrain a child if she is hurting herself or anyone else. Hold her face gently, but firmly, with both hands to make her stop and listen to you.

▶ Use hand gestures—putting your finger to your lips, touching your child on the shoulder—to guide your child's behavior. Also show approval with gestures—a smile, a wink, a handshake, a pat on the back.

If your child is having trouble responding to both verbal and nonverbal guidance, follow up some behaviors with appropriate consequences. This can be tricky. Like the problem of offering a choice where none really exists, you don't want to make a demand you are not prepared to follow through on. When you make a demand, you are really saying, *"Do as I say or else!"* The "or else" is a consequence, and you have to be ready with one if your child doesn't follow your direction.

In Early Childhood classrooms, the consequence for inappropriate behavior is often being sent away from the group for a period of time. This works really well at home, too. When you send your child to her room or just away from you, you are telling her that her behavior is unacceptable if she wants to stay with you and that she must change that behavior if she wants to be with other people. It gives her time to think about her actions in a calm place and it allows **her** to make the decision to behave appropriately and rejoin you.

Consequences can be positive, too. Praise and attention are just as valuable as treats in most cases. Special times together are perhaps the most positive reinforcements you can use. This book will give you lots of ideas for activities, outings, and projects to use as rewards.

TOGETHER

Make Aggression Cookies when you don't have a punching bag handy or the space to run off aggressive feelings. The more you pound and knead them, the better they taste!

You can also use the activities in this book to redirect troublesome behavior. It is like the distraction techniques I mentioned before; sometimes, anger, frustration, or sadness need to be channeled into some appropriate activity. Carpentry helps let off steam—even if it's only pounding golf tees into a melon rind with a mallet. Pounding a good-sized piece of clay or play dough can drive away the blues. Cooking, dancing, playing a rhythm instrument, tearing paper for a collage, drawing a scary monster with bold strokes on a large sheet of paper, all of these can help redirect hurt or angry feelings and potentially troublesome behavior into creativity.

As you now can see, discipline can be a really positive thing for your child. When discipline guides, corrects, and strengthens rather than serves as a put down, then your child is learning self-control, which in turn builds self-esteem.

AGGRESSION COOKIES

YOU'LL NEED:

3 cups oatmeal

1 1/2 cups flour

1 1/2 cups brown sugar

2 1/2 tsp. baking powder

1 1/2 cups butter

large bowl

cookie sheet

WHAT TO DO:

1. Dump ingredients into a large bowl.

2. MASH IT! POUND IT! KNEAD IT!

3. Roll dough into small balls.

4. Bake on a cookie sheet at 350°F for 10-12 minutes.

Thinking Skills

In guiding your child's behavior, you are helping her develop an important thinking skill--the ability to understand cause and effect. There are many other thinking skills that you can help your child develop. These are critically important for when she enters school and learns to read. Just as you help your child learn basic concepts by creating an environment where she can explore and discover them on her own, you can help her develop basic thinking skills by asking questions that will lead her to explore ideas and discover relationships.

Throughout this book, I will give you ideas for teaching concepts and skills in the context of the special times you spend together. But these basic thinking skills are so important that I want to introduce them here in the hope that they will be in the back of your mind whenever you are dealing with your child.

From the moment of birth, your child began to develop her thinking skills. She used all her senses to explore her world and later try to control it. In the most basic way, a baby learns to solve the problems of getting fed, cleaned up, held, and put down to sleep—to communicate its needs by crying, making special sounds and expressions.

Tell me about what you see!

Your child will solve problems throughout her life and you, as her first teacher, can help by having her learn the skills involved in problem-solving, then giving her opportunities to talk through her thought processes and test out solutions, and finally by helping her achieve that sense of satisfaction and self-confidence that comes from solving problems constructively.

Reading expert, Martha A. Hayes, points out seven basic thinking skills involved in solving problems that are also essential for learning to read. For each of these skills, there are certain basic types of questions or directions you can use everyday so that your child will have more practice using the skill. You can work these easily into your daily routines and special times together with your child when she is having new experiences and meeting new people.

The first of these important thinking skills is NOTING DETAILS. Your child uses her eyes to see details which she then should be encouraged to name and describe—using all of her senses. Try to work the following questions and directions into conversations with your child.
- *"What is the name of this thing (person, place)?"*
- *"Tell me about what you see."*
- *"What shapes do you see?"*
- *"What size do you think this is?"*
- *"Tell me something about it after you taste (touch, smell, listen to) it."*

The next skill is making COMPARISONS. Here, your child is looking at two or more things and making decisions about similarities and differences. Items may be exactly alike or have similar parts. Your child will have to be able to notice details to practice the skill of comparison. Use questions similar to these to encourage your child to compare.

"*Do these two balls look the same or are they different from each other?*"

"*What makes these two plants look alike?*"

"*What do you think is the same about these crayons?*"

"*Is this dog bigger or smaller than that one?*"

After your child has had some practice in comparison, she will begin to sort things into groups—to CLASSIFY them. Each object, person, event, or place in a group has similar characteristics or uses. As she classifies, your child is noting details and comparing. Here are some sample questions to stimulate practice in this skill.

"*Put all the clothes that are blue in one pile.*"

"*What do you call all of these objects?*" (toys, clothes, cans)

"*What is alike about all of these people?*" (red hair, dresses, glasses)

When your child is telling you a story, she is practicing SEQUENCE. Whenever she is describing a series of events in order or in the order of a sequentially arranged pattern, she is using this thinking skill. She can be describing degrees of difference within a single concept–sizes, temperature, or shading. To practice sequencing, your child has to be familiar with words which describe order, so use them often in your own speech. Also, use questions like those that follow.

- *"What happened to Goldilocks first? Next? Last?"*
- *"What comes next in this pattern–a round bead or a square one?"*
- *"In what order do you eat your sandwich and ice cream?"*
- *"Which day was the sunniest?"*

As I discussed in <u>Guiding Behavior</u>, your child will be able to understand why something happened or what will happen when she can figure out either the CAUSE or the EFFECT of an action or event. She will begin to realize that everything that occurs has a reason and a result. Talk about cause and effect with your child when you are discussing behavior and also use questions similar to the following in everyday situations.

- *"Why do you think this happened?"*

"What do you think will happen if you do this now?"
When your child makes an INFERENCE about a situation, event, or person, she is making a guess about details which she has not actually seen or filling in the gaps of information which have not been stated. She needs some background information and understanding of basic concepts if she is to "guess" correctly. Here are the types of questions that will challenge your child to make inferences.

■ *"Why do you think that Cinderella was unhappy that she wasn't invited to the ball?"*

■ *"What do we have to do to make a grilled cheese sandwich?"*

■ *"If I told you to draw a picture of a girl, what would you do?"*

When your child PREDICTS THE OUTCOME of a situation, she first uses the thinking skills of sequencing, understanding cause and effect, and making inferences about what happened. Only after that can she figure out a possible outcome or an ending to a story. Encourage her to practice this skill by asking questions like the following.

■ *"What do you think will happen next?"*

■ *"How do you think this story will end?"*

■ *"If Goldilocks falls asleep in Baby Bear's bed, what will happen when the bears come home?"*

All of the questions above set up problems for your child to solve. With them in mind, you will see lots of potential problems in your daily life and during special times that your child can solve—and feel good about herself for doing it.

Special Treasures

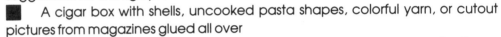

Special times offer a perfect opportunity for you to help your child practice thinking skills by collecting treasures. Mementos of special times can be the beginnings of wonderful collections–important learning experiences for your child and pleasurable memories for the whole family. Aside from gathering mementos of special trips or occasions, collecting pebbles, leaves, or even coupons from the supermarket gives your child a purpose or goal for everyday activities.

Whether it is postcards, toy cars, or things associated with a circus visit, the first thing your child has to do is to decide what will fit into her collection–the general topic or category she wants to collect. This is an exercise in classifying. Then, she has to decide where the collection will be stored. This is a problem to solve which has to do with the size of her collectibles, the size of the collection itself, and how much it will grow. Here first are some suggestions for storage places.

■ A cigar box with shells, uncooked pasta shapes, colorful yarn, or cutout pictures from magazines glued all over

■ Plastic foam egg cartons, which are great for small item collections– pebbles, buttons, seeds

■ Styrofoam meat trays with plastic wrap covers, useful for glued-down treasures

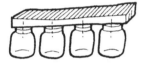

TOGETHER

Create Treasure Keepers together to hold mementos of special times.

Does your child plan to display her collection? This presents another creative problem to solve. Try any of the following. (Present her with the material and let your child try to figure out how to use it.)

■ A large shirt box with many smaller jewelry boxes glued inside to make a shadowbox

■ Baby food jars with the covers attached to a piece of wood with a nail or screw, great for displaying small collections neatly

■ Empty, cleaned bleach bottles or milk jugs with a window cut on the side for displaying and carrying the collection around

■ Baskets and tins–decorative ways to store collections that are growing and changing

Once your child actually starts collecting, she gets lots of practice in comparison. The collector has to look at each new item in terms of color, size, shape, use–any number of categories–to see if it fits into her collection. If she is collecting shells and finds a new one on a trip to the shore, she must remember what the shells in her collection are like and if this one fits in. So many thinking skills–and such fun!

Whenever you can, encourage your child to talk about her collection(s), so that you can add new words to her vocabulary. She will probably be proud to share her efforts with anyone who will take the time to look and listen. These first collections will create special times for you and your child as well as commemorate them, I promise.

TREASURE KEEPERS

WHAT TO DO:

OATMEAL BOXES

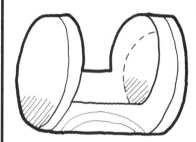

Empty oatmeal boxes can be cut down in the middle of the side so that books, records, cassettes, or magazines can be stored.

CYLINDER CONTAINERS

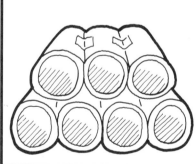

Oatmeal boxes, potato chip cans, ice cream containers, and orange juice cans make great containers for poster collections or artwork when they are taped together and laid on their sides.

CORRUGATED LIQUOR BOXES

These boxes, with cardboard sections inside, make great cubbies for some collections. You can also add 1 quart paper milk carton with 1 side cut out to use as a drawer by placing it in the cubbies and pulling out with the carton top.

Planning Special Times

Now you are ready to get into the good part—ideas for special times you can share with your child. I urge you to take along the hints from this chapter—on a hike, to the beach, to a Halloween party, to the first day of school, even to situations in times of stress. Always keep in the back of your mind the many concepts, skills, and behaviors your child is learning during her first six years. Think about that most important attitude she needs to develop—self-confidence. And remember that during special times when she is often bombarded with new experiences and people, your child needs as much support and encouragement as possible.

When you are planning your special times, let your child participate as much as possible. When a weekend outing comes up, let her have the opportunity and the responsibility for making plans. This involves making choices and problem-solving.

If you have a free weekend or only an afternoon with nothing planned, try a family brainstorming session or a one-on-one discussion with your child. Brainstorming encourages creative thinking. Many businesses use it for solving problems and coming up with new ideas. On a junior level, many kindergartens are beginning to build brainstorming into their curriculum. So you can never start practicing this skill too early with your child. Introduce a problem and encourage everyone to come up with as many solutions as they can. The only ground rules are:

■   All ideas are accepted, no matter how crazy they may seem; in fact, the more ideas the better. You should end up with a great variety of solutions, one of which will turn out to be the best solution or will be combined with another idea or improved upon. One person's idea can trigger a different thought in someone else.

■   No one may criticize or even discuss someone else's idea while you are brainstorming. Everyone, especially the young child or children in the group, should feel that their contributions are important.

So your stated problem is, *"What shall we do next Saturday afternoon?"* Once you have finished brainstorming alternatives, talked about the feasibility of the different ideas (weather, transportation, appropriateness for the group as a whole), and chosen the best solution, let your child help you plan clothing, food, tickets—whatever is necessary to make your plans a reality.

Circle the date on the calendar and let your child mark off the days. At this stage of her life, she needs something concrete to give her the sense of time passing. If an outing is more than you can plan ahead for, try an "afternoon of fun." You might let your child choose a project from the TOGETHER pages in this book. Then, together, plan the materials you will need (details) Talk about where you will do the activity and when(inference), the steps needed to complete the project(sequence), and perhaps why your child chose the effect) Don't forget to talk about concepts like colors, shapes, numbers, and letters as you work together.

On outings, talk about the "new worlds" your child is exploring. Suggest some of the following. A zoo is one kind of world where animals live in special homes, eating special foods with special rules. A museum is a totally different world with a different set of things to experience and rules of behavior to follow. Encourage your child to explore with all of her senses; let her discover the sights, sounds, tastes, and smells of each experience. This can make going to the supermarket as much of a learning adventure as visiting a nature preserve or an amusement park.

Be careful, however: don't make it seem like work. Don't let your child think there are right and wrong answers to the questions you ask. Keep the conversations informal, fun, and interesting. Again, the most important part of any special time you share with your child is the potential for your child to grow—in self-esteem, self-discipline, development of concepts and skills, in the love of learning—and in her relationship with you.

WEEKENDS

2

Saturdays and Sundays

Weekends are special times in most families. Everyone—including the children—works hard during the week and looks forward to relaxing and spending time together Saturday and Sunday. If you are a parent who works outside the home, this may be the only time you have to really "enjoy" your child. If you are the noncustodial parent of a divorced family, you may need the weekend to reconnect with your child and deal with the many issues of separation.

Most families don't have the luxury of "playing" all weekend—every weekend. Parents, especially, have chores to do around the house and other outside obligations, so often "special times" must be short. This chapter begins with ideas that take no more than 20 minutes to have fun.

Along with time, another variable is the weather. There are suggestions in this chapter that are appropriate for different seasons of the year and all types of weather. There is a whole chapter on summer, starting on page 65.

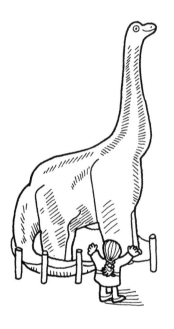

Finally, there are general suggestions for weekend excursions. You know the places to go in your area and the local newspaper will tell you about all the special events for children. As you are looking over the possibilities, I would suggest that you find an excursion that you AND your child will enjoy. The most valuable time you spend together is the time when you are both having fun.

Luckily, children are interested in just about everything. Don't feel that your trip to the museum is a failure if all your child talks about when you get home is the men cleaning a statue. That is what interested him the most and was a learning experience for him.

Most young children have short attention spans. If the museum is close to your home, it is preferable to plan a short—no more than 45 minutes—visit to the Costume Collection and return another time to see the Dinosaur Room. In the same way, it is better to arrive just before curtain time at a play or concert than to make your child sit quietly for 20 minutes with nothing to do until the curtain goes up.

Before you leave on an excursion, be sure to tell your child exactly what you will be doing. *"We will drive to the museum, look at the pretty clothes that people wore long ago, go to a restaurant for pizza, and then come home."* Children feel more secure and confident when they know the agenda, especially in new situations.

Enjoy your weekend adventures—both the long and the short ones. Cherish every special time.

Take a Walk

Sometimes you just don't have the time to take a daylong or even an afternoon excursion with your child on a weekend. But, how about a walk together? In 20 minutes, you can stretch your legs, get your heart pumping vigorously, and have an exciting learning experience with your child. You don't have to go far. Choose a destination that is five minutes away from your home. Plan to spend 10 minutes at the special place—exploring, making collections, or playing a game. Your child may even wish to collect items for follow-up projects at home. Then, walk back for five minutes and you've had a "special time" together. Your child will have the opportunity to develop his observation skills and also to learn some important concepts.

At least four times in the year, take a walk to observe signs of the season. Encourage your child to take in the changes in nature and the environment with all of his senses. For example, in the early spring, put on your sweaters and go out to discover signs of spring. Before you leave home, say to your your child, *This is the beginning of spring. Let's go out and see what has changed from winter."* Of course, look for the special changes that occur in your part of the country. Here are some general ideas for things to observe.

▶ Look for buds on trees and bushes. Encourage your child to search for those first green blades of grass. He may have to get down on the ground and really explore with a hand lens.

▶ Have your child find a new dandelion plant in a sheltered place. Insert a popsicle stick in the earth next to the plant. Mark how high the plant is. The following week, walk back to the plant and again mark its height. Check its growth for a few weeks in a row.

▶ Look for spring blossoms: pussywillow, cherry, apple, and forsythia—you can take budding branches inside, put them in water, and they will blossom in one to two weeks.

▶ Encourage your child to observe the colors of spring. Make a chart for him, writing the names of the eight basic colors in the appropriate crayons on a piece of paper. Attach to a small clipboard with a pencil tied to the board with a string. Challenge your child to make a tally mark for each color he sees.

 Keep a chart for each season of the year. Compare the results and talk about the colors of different objects. See if some objects change color in different seasons.

▶ Look for birds associated with spring in your area. They will be building nests at this time of year; watch as they collect materials. Your child can help the birds in their search for materials by filling a mesh onion bag with pieces of colored yarn and hanging the bag on a tree. Birds will pull the yarn out of the bag and use it to build their nests. On a spring walk, look up and see if you can find some of your yarn in various nests in the trees.

■ Listen to the sounds of birds, insects and animals. Hear frogs croaking, if you are near a pond. You might even hear the sound of distant thunder from a spring storm.

■ Smell the moist earth, the fresh spring air—before and after a rain shower—the onion grass, the different scents of the spring flowers.

TOGETHER

Create some clever Collection Containers to make collenting samples easy.

Feel the change in temperature as the season changes. Place a thermometer in the shade as you leave for your walk. Check it when you return and then place the thermometer in the sun and observe what happens. Talk about why the temperature changes.

Have your child decide whether the things he observes on his walk are old or new. These are important concepts for young children to learn. For example, buds are new, but the big trees on which they are found are old.

If you live in a neighborhood with a lot of houses or apartment buildings, check for signs of spring cleaning. Do a little spring cleaning of your own on your walk. Give your child a paper bag to carry along and instruct him to pick up papers and "not too dirty" litter. Show him how to dispose of it properly.

Other Walks

Country, suburbs, or city—wherever you live—there are exciting, fun-filled, educational walks you can take with your child. Your child can keep tally cards of many things:

■ Colors of cars that pass on the road.

■ Types of houses you pass (brick, wood, metal siding). You might want to read The Three Little Pigs before you take this walk.

■ Numbers of people—children, men, or women—or even pets you pass

■ Signs that you see. Your child may be able to write down some of the words.

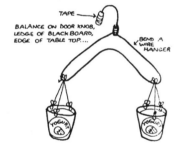

TAPE
BALANCE ON DOOR KNOB, LEDGE OF BLACK BOARD, EDGE OF TABLE TOP....
BEND A WIRE HANGER

Fall Walks

Fall is an excellent time to take walks and collect items to bring home for projects. Have your child collect a good quantity of acorns, seed pods, sunflower seeds, and other natural fall items for learning experiences. When you get home from your walks, try these math games.

Provide a balance scale—two yogurt containers suspended from a wire hanger with thread—for your child to compare the various weights of the objects.

Provide empty egg cartons for your child to sort his finds.

Have your child use groups of the same type of objects for counting.

Encourage your child to put three or four of the same type of object—leaves, pods, gourds—in size order.

Your child can also use his fall items to learn about letters and language experience.

Make a large alphabet chart. Have your child add a fall item found on a walk to each section. For example, A—acorn; P—pumpkin seed.

Make booklets in fall shapes—leaves, apples, pumpkins—and let your child paste in fall items and then dictate or write stories about them.

COLLECTION CONTAINERS

1. PLASTIC MILK CONTAINER

Child can tuck handle into a belt and wear it

cut out a hole

2. HANGING COTTAGE CHEESE CONTAINER

yarn

COTTAGE CHEESE

Child can suspend yarn around his neck

Use container to collect nuts, leaves, etc

3. PAPER MILK CARTON CONTAINER

pipe cleaners

½ paper milk carton

MILK

Child hangs container from his wrist.

4. NYLON STOCKING NET

Nylon stocking sewed on wire hanger

Twist "hook" of wire hanger to form a handle

5. KNAPSACK

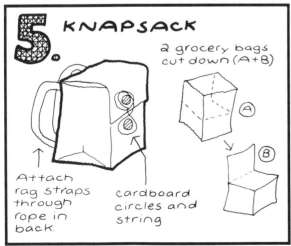

2 grocery bags cut down (A+B)

Ⓐ

Ⓑ

Attach rag straps through rope in back.

cardboard circles and string

6. ZIP LOCKING PLASTIC BAGS

Stitch zip locking bags together along left side and string with heavy piece of twine.

Child can wear it over head and shoulders.

Open bags to put in samples.

Of course, fall treasures lend themselves to marvelous art experiences.

▶ Let your child print with leaves, fruit and vegetable sections, and various pods. Have him use watercolors and brayers.

▶ Older children enjoy making seed jewelry. Soak pumpkin seeds in water for half an hour and let your child string them on heavy thread with a blunt needle.

▶ Hang a two-feet by three-feet piece of burlap from a wooden dowel. Pull a few horizontal threads. Let your child weave pods, feathers, leaves, cornstalks, and other natural items in the burlap to create an autumn wall hanging.

▶ Let your child paint with natural colors. Have him pick berries-- blueberries and raspberries—and then crush them with a wooden spoon in a plastic container. Add a few drops of vinegar to prevent mold from forming. Let him paint with brushes or write using a stick pen.

▶ Help your child make a nature mask with materials found on a walk. If you live in an area where leaves shed their bark, bring some home to use as the background for a mask.

Winter Fun

Depending on where you live, you may not be taking too many walks in the winter; but it's fun for your child to play outside in the snow. While you are shoveling the driveway, your child can make a maze for you. Mark a starting place and let your child walk in all different directions to a finishing place that you have designated. When you're finished your chores, see if you can get through the maze. Two or more children can have knee races in the snow with their snowsuits on. They will love seeing who can go the fastest "running" on his knees. There are more ideas for fun outside on page 38.

It's even more fun sometimes to relax inside with hot chocolate and do some winter-related projects on a snowy weekend. You'll find creative ideas on page 39.

TOGETHER

Collect flowers and leaves on a walk to make Potpourri. Use it to create wonderful holiday gifts.

POT POURRI

YOU'LL NEED

 jar with lid

bowl

teaspoon

 orrisroot (available in drug stores and health food stores)

 measuring cup

 Flower petals and leaves- roses, violets, jasmine, narcissus

 herbs- basil leaves, sage, thyme, lavender, lemon verbena

 OPTIONAL: spices, cloves, allspice, or cinnamon

WHAT TO DO:

1. Collect flower petals and leaves- roses, violets, jasmine, narcissus.

2. Pick herbs- sage, basil leaves, thyme, lavender, lemon verbena.

3. Dry petals and herbs on paper in an airy, dry place- out of the sunlight.

4. When dry, mix in a bowl with 1 tsp. of orrisroot to each pint of petals.

5. Add spices, if you wish- cloves, cinnamon, or allspice.

6. Put mixture in a tightly covered jar for 6 weeks. Then, open and make into little pillows or keep in baskets.

FUN IN THE COLD

Fill various size paper milk containers with water. Set outside in freezing temperatures. Leave overnight. Tear away paper containers. Assemble frozen blocks into a fort or other building.

Child and adult fill balloon and plastic glove with water and secure tightly with elastic bands. Place outside in freezing temperatures. Tear away plastic. Use for decorations.

Put diluted food coloring in an empty, rinsed out spray bottle. Spray colors on the ground to make designs in clean, white snow.

FUN OUT OF THE SNOW

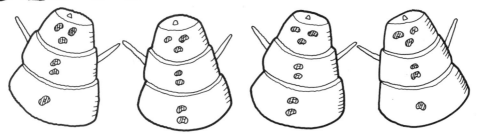

SNOWY DAY PICTURES

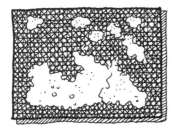

1. Have children mix Ivory Snow Flakes and water with handbeaters until thick and foamy.

2. Then, let them paint with this mixture on blue paper to create a snowy scene.

SNOWMAN SNACKS

1. Provide each child with 3 marshmallows and a toothpick.

2. Let them build model snowmen and add raisins for facial features and buttons.

3. Extra toothpicks can be used for arms.

ICE CRYSTAL PICTURES

1. Have children draw a picture with crayons on a darkish piece of construction paper.

2. Prepare a mixture of equal parts of epsom salts and water.

3. Have children paint the solution over their crayon picture. When paper dries, "ice crystals" will appear.

W eather For e casts

Stuck for something special to do on a weekend? Sometimes the weather forecast can give you some ideas. Just looking up in the sky can spark the imagination.

Sunny Days

Sunny days give you and your child the opportunity to enjoy the out-of-doors. Has your child ever asked **why** the sky is blue? When he does, you can do the following experiment together to find out. You'll need a glass of water, some milk, and a flashlight. First, stir a few drops of milk into the glass of water. Darken the room and shine the flashlight on the side of the glass. Let your child look through the side of the glass. The liquid looks bluish, not white. The drops of milk have scattered the blue light rays. Talk about how the drops of milk in the water scatter the blue light rays from the flashlight in the same way specks of dust and water in the air scatter the light rays from the sun. The sky looks blue because the blue light rays scatter the most.

On a sunny day, consider taking a camera walk with your child. Photography is an important part of our lives today. There is no reason why it shouldn't be part of our children's lives, too. With the proper introduction, a preschooler can learn to take pictures with an inexpensive camera. Of course, the most effective type of camera for a young child is one that gives instant gratification–the instant developing kind–but there are so many places today that have one-hour or overnight developing service for regular film that it seems silly to spend all of that extra money on special film.

TOGETHER

Make a Photostory Book with your child to save his pictures.

Your child's first camera adventure might take place in your own backyard. Very likely, his first subjects will include you, his house, and the family pet. Then, consider going on a photo safari one sunny day to bring back pictures with a specific theme.   Many themes will provide exciting learning experiences for your child. Let him choose one that appeals before you set out. His choice may dictate where you go to take the pictures. Here are some suggestions.

- Natural objects and the sky
- Objects in special colors
- Words on street signs, billboards, and on storefronts
- Objects of special shapes
- Interesting people–old, young, male, female, groups of people

The list can go on and on. If your child comes up with a theme, that's creative thinking.   When he chooses the items to take pictures of, he is using classification skills.

Another fun photo safari involves the making of a photostory book. Let your child take pictures of events in his day. When the snapshots are developed, let him select specific ones to tell the story of the day. Here he is using his recall skills. Next, encourage him to arrange the pictures in sequential order.

PHOTOSTORY BOOK

YOU'LL NEED:

1 piece of fabric, 11½"x17½"
(use pinking shears
to cut edges.)

 paste

 permanent marker

 hole puncher

 5 pieces, 8½"x11" typing paper

 clear, contact paper

yarn and yarn needle

WHAT TO DO:

1.
Make the book with 5 pages folded in half on inside and fabric folded in half for outside cover.

2.
Punch 2 holes near fold on each page.

3.
Insert yarn through cover and holes. Tie with a bow.

4.
Write child's name and date of "photosafari" on the cover.

Sara's weekend

May 23-24, 1987

5.
Have child arrange photographs in sequential order.

6.
Glue photographs onto pages.

7.
Have child dictate or write descriptions or comments under each photograph.

8.
Cover each page with clear contact paper.

Cloudy Days

Cloudy days are full of fun and learning. Clouds stimulate experiences for your child with science language, art, and creative thinking. Start off your cloudy day together by reading one of many wonderful books for children about clouds. Try Dreams by Peter Spier and Clouds by Kanzo Nizaka.

A good book can send your child to the window or outside where he can lie flat on his back and make his own observations. Once he starts cloud watching, your inquisitive child will probably want to know what a cloud is. It is tiny drops of water or ice that hang together in the sky. Moisture in the air forms clouds. Remind your child that when he breathes out in winter, often he can see his breath because the cold air instantly cools the moisture from his mouth. Clouds are formed in very much the same way.

Tell your child that looking at the clouds can help him tell what kind of weather to expect. High puffy clouds usually signal good weather, while low, dark, heavy-looking clouds may mean that rain is on the way. The names of the clouds are long and complicated, so don't bother trying to teach them to your child unless he is the type that thrives on names like "brontosaurus."

On a nice day, spread a blanket in the backyard or in the park and lie down with your child to observe the clouds. Point out how they are always moving and changing formations. Encourage your child to tell you what they look like to him.

Back inside, let your child create pictures of clouds using cotton balls dipped in glue. Or, make the recipe for paint on page 39 for your child to use with a brush or as fingerpaint.

Windy Days

Your child can see the clouds, but, he cannot see the wind--only the effects of its power. He can, however, feel the wind.

Go outside on a windy day and encourage your child to experience the difference in walking into and away from the wind. When he closes his eyes, ask if he feels as though someone is pushing him. Bring out some crepe paper streamers or long scarves and let him "run with the wind."

TOGETHER

Make a simple kite to enjoy on a windy day. Read Let's Make a Kite by Jack Stokes.

Let your child experience the wind at ground level. Then, go to a higher place so you both can see how it feels. Have him drop things like feathers, paper, a rock, and a plastic toy. Have your child observe what happens to each object. After a while, have him predict what will happen to an object before you drop it. Also discuss with your child how clouds are moved by the wind and how this changes our weather patterns. You might want to look at the book Why Kites Fly, The Story of the Wind at Work by Don Dwiggins. Read together Gilberto and the Wind by Marie Hall Ets.

MAKE A KITE

YOU'LL NEED:

string

scissors

hole punch

heavyweight plastic trash bags or empty plastic bread wrappers

fabric scraps

permanent felt tip markers

WHAT TO DO:

1.
Punch a hole in 1 side of the bag opening. Attach a long string.

2.
Tie 6" strips of plastic or lightweight fabric to a 15" long piece of string or thinner piece of plastic for the streamer.

3.
Decorate with markers or "enjoy" the colors of the advertisements on the wrappers.

Rainy Days and Sundays

There are activities throughout this book that can be done on rainy weekends. The main idea is to have a variety of ideas and projects–some active, some quiet–to meet the changing moods and short attention span of your young child.

Balloons

It can be difficult to find activities that are active and work well inside. Why not try some fun and learning with balloons? Children of all ages love balloons. No matter where they are, they make you think of parties and parades.

wire hanger

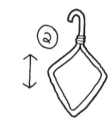
nylon stocking

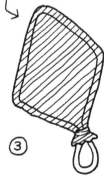

BALLOON PADDLE

Buy some eight-inch round party balloons. They are easier to inflate and larger than the standard variety, so they are somewhat easier to control. On the next rainy weekend, find a large, relatively clutter-free space and try some of the following activities.

▶ Attach a pair of oaktag feet to a balloon. When your child bats the balloon in the air, it will land on its "feet" every time.

▶ Inflate a balloon, let it go, and watch it zoom around the room as the air escapes.

▶ Have your child tap a balloon in the air using one hand, both hands, left and right hands, his head, and knees. This can become a game of "Simon Says" with a group.

▶ Encourage your child to lie on his back and tap a balloon in the air. Let him try to tap it with his feet.

▶ You can help your child practice his number skills if you call out a number and have him hit his balloon that number of times.

▶ Introduce your child to the game "Paddle Balloon." In advance, bend a wire clothes hanger into as circular a shape as possible. Bend the hook at the end so it resembles the handle of a paddle. Slip a pantyhose leg over the circular frame and tape the stocking to the handle securely. This paddle is excellent for batting balloons. It provides a fun way to help your child work on his hand-eye coordination. The paddle can be used to tap the balloon in the air or back and forth with a partner.

▶ If your child doesn't mind the noise of a popping balloon, you might want to put a little message in the balloon before you blow it up. Let him pop it and "read" the message at the end of playtime.

▶ Stretch your child's imagination by having him pretend to be a balloon after playing with one. Tell him, *"You are a balloon and someone is blowing you up. You are getting bigger and bigger, rounder and rounder. Now you are all blown up and you can move gently around the room. You are light as air. Oh dear! Someone has popped you with a pin. All the air rushes out of you and you sink to the ground."* This is an excellent way to make the transition from active balloon play to a quieter activity.

▶ Another transition might be reading a story together like Pa's Balloon and Other Pig Tales by Arthur Geisert or The Great Valentine's Day Balloon Race by Adrienne Adams.

Rainbows

What better thing to think about on a rainy weekend than the end of the dull, gray day and the coming of the sun? Rainbows symbolize that ending. The gold at the end of the rainbow is the sunshine that hides behind the dark, gloomy clouds. Maybe if you plan some rainbow-inspired activities inside on a rainy day, a real rainbow will appear outside your window.

Always look for a rainbow on a rainy day when the sun suddenly appears. Have your child look into the sky in the opposite position from where the sun is shining. He may see a rainbow if there is still moisture in the air.

You can create a rainbow for your child inside with a deep, clear dish or glass of water and a mirror. Set the glass in the sunlight. Place the mirror in water so that the mirror is leaning on the glass and the sun's rays are reflected off of it through the water onto a blank wall. When the water becomes still, there will be a lovely rainbow on the wall.

Rainbows offer you the opportunity to explore color with your child. A child's first approach to color is exploratory. Young children do not draw purple cows because they see cows that are purple; rather they like the color purple and enjoy exploring with it. Suns, houses, dogs, even Mom and Dad, may be purple until the child tires of that color and goes on to another.

Talk with your child about the colors in a rainbow. Have him choose his favorite—of the moment—and do a one-color picture, perhaps using crayons of different shades. If you have some magazines around, he might like to do a one-color collage. If he likes to dress up, help him find enough articles of clothing to wear a one-color outfit.

In preschool programs, young children play matching and sorting games to learn about colors. You can play similar games at home with your child on a rainy day. Place sheets of construction paper, one in each of the basic colors, on the floor or on a table. Challenge your child to find objects in each color and place them on the appropriate sheet. This is an excellent activity for your child to do independently. You can work or relax nearby.

Give your child objects to sort by color. If you sew, you may have enough buttons to create a challenging game for your child. Give him an empty egg carton to hold the groups. Your child can also sort socks, shirts, cans in the kitchen, seed packets in spring—once you start looking, you'll find many ideas around the house.

Back to the original rainbows. If your child is older and proficient at color recognition, try stimulating his creative thinking skills by asking him to draw a picture of a rainbow and what is "over the rainbow" and "under" it. A rainy day is a wonderful time to read the book and/or rent the videotape of *The Wizard of Oz*. You will also enjoy reading Eric Carle's delightful I See a Song.

Enjoy different art media as you try Six Ways to Make a Rainbow on the following two pages.

6 WAYS TO MAKE A RAINBOW

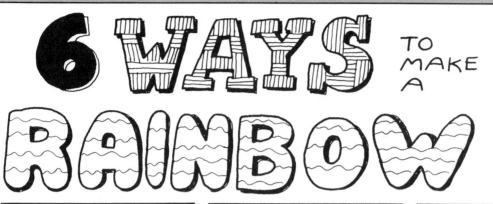

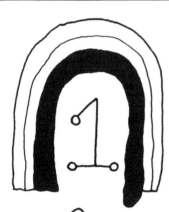

A FINGER PAINT RAINBOW

Into a large bowl, put 1 cup mild laundry soap powder, 1 cup dry powder or chip starch, and 1 cup water. Beat with a rotary beater until thick. Divide into small bowls and add food colors.

food colors

small bowls

A WET CHALK RAINBOW

Soak pieces of colored chalk for about 5 minutes in a styrofoam meat tray. Use chalk on its side for a dramatic effect.

A CRAYON SHAVING RAINBOW

Use a cheese grater and grate broken crayons. keep colors separate. (Adult cleans grater in boiling water.) Sprinkle into rainbow form on waxed paper. Cover with another piece of waxed paper. Place on folded old newspapers. Cover with a sheet of plain paper. Iron.

iron
paper
waxed paper
waxed paper

grated crayons

folded newspaper

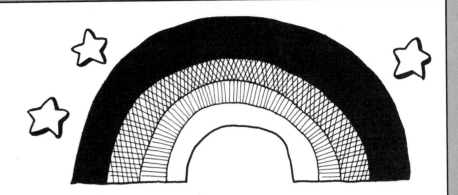

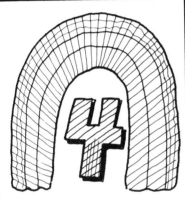

A WATER COLOR RAINBOW

Paint a rainbow with watercolor paints.
(Experiment by first wetting paper with water.)

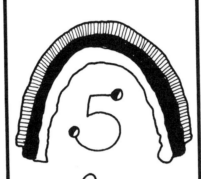

A PAPER-PEELED CRAYON RAINBOW

Draw a rainbow by holding a paper-peeled crayon on its side. Use a different color for each rainbow stripe.

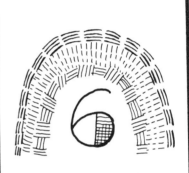

A COLORED RICE RAINBOW

Dye white rice by using a few drops of food color in a plastic bag. Shake well. Spread colored rice out to dry on a paper towel. When dry, glue onto cardboard.

In the Kitchen

A rainy weekend afternoon is the perfect time to be creative in the kitchen. And, when you are not under pressure to get a meal on the table, you have the time and space to let your child be the star chef.

There are so many things your child can learn while involved in the cooking process. He is developing all of the important thinking skills:

■ Detail—what is needed for a recipe
■ Comparison—raw/cooked; hot/cold; frozen/unfrozen
■ Classification—food; utensils; fruits; vegetables
■ Sequence—following a recipe; making a sandwich; toasting bread
■ Cause and effect—making ice cubes; greasing a cookie sheet; pricking a baking potato
■ Inference—what it takes to make batter into pancakes; where to keep the ice cream in the refrigerator
■ Predicting outcomes—a teakettle is heated; a cake is put in the oven

Your child also develops small motor coordination in the kitchen. Grinding, spreading, rolling, beating, slicing, mashing, and grating--all of these actions give your child important motor skill practice.

There are a few no-fail things your child can make in the kitchen that will give him freedom and self-confidence. They are perfect weekend projects.

▶ FRUIT SALADS allow him to mix any number of fruits with spectacular results.

▶ VEGETABLE SOUP is much the same as fruit salad--the more ingredients, the better. Start with a chicken soup base. Stay away from beets and salad greens, but let your child add all of the cooked pasta and rice he likes.

▶ BLENDER SHAKES are lots of fun for your child to create. Have him start with milk and add fruit, ice cream, cookie crumbs, nuts, or whatever appeals to him. Challenge him to tell you which of all of the separate ingredients he can taste once they are blended together.

▶ BREAD AND PRETZEL DOUGHS are terrific for your child to roll, pull, mold, and so on. Use frozen bread dough, your favorite recipe, or the recipe for CELEBRATION BREAD on pages 100 and 101.

▶ BREAD PUDDING can be made from your bread leftovers. Have your child tear the bread into small pieces. Place in an ovenproof bowl and let your child add three or four eggs, two or three cups of milk, a dash of salt, and sugar or honey to taste. Then, he can mix the ingredients well with a wooden spoon. Add spices, like cinnamon or nutmeg, lemon rind, raisins, apple slices, or nuts. Bake at 325 degrees until set.

Let your child help in the kitchen not only on weekends, but whenever you are preparing meals. Take a few moments before you begin to think about jobs he can do. It will make him feel useful and self-confident, rather than left-out and cranky. And, it will help him develop basic skills and concepts.

TOGETHER

Wok recipes are fun and quick to prepare. The whole family can participate. Your child can help you cut the vegetables.

WOK, DON'T RUN!

The WOK, the simple Chinese cooking pan, allows for very fast cooking with a minimum of fats and an emphasis on crunchy vegetables. Another nice factor is that you can vary ingredients and use items you have on hand.

General Cooking Method

Heat the wok on the stove until very hot. Add 2 Tblsp. OIL (peanut, vegetable) and swirl over inside of pan. Add VEGETABLES first and stir fry them for 3-5 minutes. You might want to add a thin slice of fresh GINGER to the vegetables.

Remove vegetables to a serving plate. Add 2 Tblsp. OIL and stir fry the MEAT, adding a CLOVE OF GARLIC, if desired. Put vegetables back into pan with the meat and add this SAUCE:

  2 Tblsp. cornstarch   1/2 cup cold water   1/4 cup soy sauce    2-3 Tblsp. honey    OPTIONAL: 2 Tblsp. sherry or wine

Cook until sauce thickens. Serve hot with rice, fried bean threads, or noodles.

COMBINATIONS
TO TRY

1.
- boneless chicken cubes
- broccoli flowerettes
- water chestnuts
- pea pods
- sesame seed garnish

2.
- thin beef strips
- water chestnuts
- pea pods
- green pepper strips

3.
- thin beef strips
- frozen French style green beans
- green onions

4.
- frozen shrimp salad
- frozen green peas
- water chestnuts

Saturday Evening

One weekend night before your child goes to sleep, read <u>The Berenstain Bears and Too Much TV</u> by Stan and Jan Berenstain to your child. At one point in the story, the bear family goes outside to watch the stars come out. Suggest that your family might do the same thing the following night. It is a wonderful experience your child will want to repeat many times.

Either take a walk or sit outside and experience the night with all your senses. Here are some suggestions to guide your child in this special experience.

▶ Talk about the darkness. *"Is night the same as a dark room?"* Be sure that your child notices how much more he can see after his eyes have adjusted to the darkness.

▶ Listen to the sounds of the night—the animals, birds, insects, people, cars, sirens, bells. If you are lucky, perhaps you can listen to the silence of the night.

▶ Help your child find the moon, some stars, and even a planet. (As a rule, planets are found slightly above the horizon in the very early evening or just before sunrise. Also, stars appear to twinkle in the sky while the planets seem to shine.) Don't let your child forget to wish on the first star he sees. (*"Star light, star bright, first star I see tonight..."*)

▶ Watch for falling stars, which are really meteors that have entered our atmosphere.

▶ Point out to your child how clouds sometimes cover the moon and stars. Tell your child that constellations are groups of stars. Long ago, people decided that these groups looked like the outlines of specific objects or people, so they gave them names. Pick out a familiar one—the Big Dipper and the Little Dipper are usually visible—and show it to your child. You might want to take a book like <u>Do You Know About the Stars?</u> by Mae Blacker Freeman or <u>The Big Dipper</u> by Franklyn Branley outside with you for reference.

  Bring a paper towel roll outside and let your child use it as a telescope. You will be surprised how much you can see without the surrounding light.

You and your child can play some games in the darkness, too.

▶ Play shadow tag in the moonlight. You can trace your child's shadow on a large piece of paper, using the moon for light.

▶ Bring some colored objects—socks, hankerchiefs, blocks—and have your child try to sort them by color in the moonlight. He will find that in the pale light of the moon, he sees things only as black or pale gray with very little or no coloring.

When you come back inside, read a soothing bedtime story like:
■ <u>Close Your Eyes</u> by Jean Marzollo
■ <u>Peterkin Meets a Star</u> by Emilie Boon
■ <u>Goodnight Moon</u> by Margaret Wise Brown

TOGETHER

Replicate the Stars you saw, using interesting materials.

STARS

PIPE CLEANER STARS

Bend pipe cleaners into star shapes and cover 1 side with glue. Place a piece of colored cellophane over the glue and let dry. When dried, trim the edges of the cellophane away from outside of pipe cleaner. Make many and hang in a window.

GRASS SEED STARS

Use a moist star-shaped sponge set on a shallow plate filled with water to grow grass seed. Keep the sponge and seeds covered with plastic in a dimly lit place until the seeds sprout. Then, place in full sunlight without the cover until grass grows thick.

TOOTHPICK STARS

Snap 5 toothpicks in half but NOT into 2 pieces. Place the snapped toothpicks into a dish with the broken parts touching in the middle. With a sponge, squeeze a few drops of water just onto the broken center. Watch as the water swells the wood and the toothpick pieces become a 5 pointed star.

Hiking

Hiking is a sport that children and adults can share. There are sure to be parks and nature centers in your area. You can find them in your local Yellow Pages. A camping store will recommend good trails for family treks and sell you the appropriate maps.

Another plus is that hiking is not a very expensive sport. The only must is a First Aid kit. Sneakers—old, comfortable ones—are fine for most family hikes. The only other equipment all the hikers should have are sunglasses and a wide brim hat for the sun, poncho in case of rain, sandwich lunch and unbreakable cup, and small backpack to store the equipment. Adults can also carry canteens or thermoses; butane lighter; pocketknife; flashlight; compass; insect repellant; toilet paper; suntan lotion; and snakebite kit.

Walk the trail you are going on before you take your child. Look out for hazards such as large brambly bushes. Also look for interesting things like wildflowers, birds' nests, and old gnarly trees or stumps with rings your child can count. Try to find a meadow, pond, or stream, where everyone can relax and your child can do some independent exploration.

How far can young children walk? It depends on the child, but no more than three miles in a day. And that may mean stopping every 15 minutes for a 10 minute rest. Whenever you are with young children, forget about the endurance contest—the idea is to have fun. Keep your goals within your sight—a stream, an ant hill, a berry patch—and be sure to have small snacks and toys to bring out during rest periods.

If you have found a meadow off the trail to explore, bring along a copy of Over in the Meadow—either the Ezra Jack Keats or the John Langstaff edition. Your child may not find many of the wildlife mentioned in the story, but it will give him an idea of what lives in a meadow. When you arrive, let him look for butterflies, insects, and birds. Bring along field guides and see if together you can identify the birds you see and all the wildflowers around. Bring along a hand lens for your child to use in exploring each specimen.

If there is a pond nearby, explore it together. In the spring, look for frog eggs, polliwogs, and tadpoles in various stages of development. If the weather is warm, a turtle may be sunning itself on a rock at the edge of the pond. Stay clear of turtles away from the edge. They may be snapping turtles. Help your child discover the many types of water bugs in or near the pond.

Back on the trail, on the way home, your child may be hot, tired, and need some diversion. Try telling some fairy tales—especially ones that take place in the woods—and weave the scenery into your story.

When you get home, try to write down some of your child's favorite memories from the hike. He can illustrate them and you will have a permanent memory of a wonderful day.

Biking

Another fun family sport is bicycling. From a very early age, children love to get around on trikes and it's only a short distance to training wheels, and then to the real thing.

If you are planning a bike outing with a very young child, it is best to have him ride in a molded plastic seat on the back of your bike. Choose a destination before you leave. Only plan to go a short distance to prevent "boredom in the back." Also, plan something active for your child to do when you reach your destination. He will want to stretch his legs as much as you want to rest yours. Plan a picnic or bring along some snacks to share at rest stops.

Do some simple warm-up exercises before you go to prevent fatigue and cramping. Be sure that you and your passenger wear hats and cover yourselves with suntan or sunscreen lotion.

Also, check out your bike to see that it is in good shape before you head out. Explain to your child what you are looking at—tires properly inflated; nuts, bolts, and screws tightly fastened; chain clean and lubricated; mirror and light clean.

Your child should begin taking responsibility for his own trike or bike as soon as he is able. Besides inspecting his vehicle, he should be responsible for cleaning and polishing it. It is important to keep bikes as free from dirt and mud as possible. He should not use soap and water as these help rust to form. Keep a collection of old rags handy for your child to use.

Here are some safety rules your child should observe as soon he begins riding on his own.

- One person on one bike—no passengers
- Bike riding ONLY in areas you designate
- Sit down while riding
- Always be careful to watch for pedestrians and immovable objects

Teach your child the standard arm signals for making turns—left arm straight out for left-hand turn; left arm bent down for right-hand turn; and left arm bent up for stopping. Practice these together.

When you are out with your child, point out the cyclists. Have your child observe how they obey the rules of the road. *"Are they riding fast or slow? Are they riding with or against the traffic? Are they wearing helmets?"*

For a change of pace, if you have room outside, create a bicycle obstacle course for your child. Use milk crates and old chairs for obstacles and try to plan a course that goes up and down so your child gets practice in all of these skills. Before you know it, the whole family will be grabbing their helmets on a sunny Saturday and heading off for a day of exercise and fun.

A Trip to the Zoo

Nice weather, family outings, and the zoo go together. More than 125 million people visit zoos and aquariums annually, making them the most popular attractions in the United States. What better way to spend a special time together?

Planning

A trip to the zoo can be a spur-of-the-moment decision, but it is even more fun with a little planning. You may have to make a few calls to find out what zoos are available in your area. Try to choose one with zoo animals, a petting zoo, places to have a picnic, and some playground equipment.

Choose a date, but don't tell your child until a week beforehand. Young children have a hard time "anticipating an event" for a long time. Put the picture of a zoo animal on your calendar and let your child mark off the days as they pass.

During the week, take your child to the library and look up zoo animals in the card catalog together. Take out some books to read before and after your trip. Here are some suggested titles.
- Animals in the Zoo by H. A. Rey
- If I Ran the Zoo by Dr. Seuss
- A Children's Zoo by Tana Hoban
- Curious George Visits the Zoo by Margaret Rey

Read and reread these books together before you go to the zoo to learn the names of some of the animals and also to raise questions about them that you may be able to answer on the trip. You might want to write these down so that your child doesn't forget them on the big day.

The day before the trip, ask your child to give you a list of animals he thinks that he might see. Write the words for him and give him the list to bring along and check as he sees the animals. If you have some old magazines, let your child cut out pictures of zoo animals. He can take the pictures to the zoo and find the real animals.

The Trip

Check the weather forecast and get ready to go. Take a change of clothes for your child and raingear for everyone if there is even a hint of bad weather. Let your child help you plan, prepare, and pack a picnic. There are suggestions on page 69. Include a first-aid kit and an instant-developing camera, as well, in your bag or backpack.

In the car on the way to the zoo, try singing *"Old MacDonald Had a Zoo."* When you arrive, take a slow walk around half the zoo. Talk about the names of the animals, how they live, the sounds they make, how they smell, what they look like—sizes, colors, skin or fur, facial features—number of babies,

TOGETHER

If rain washes out your trip to the zoo, try making some of these Animal Constructions with your child. They make great follow-up projects, too.

ANIMAL CONSTRUCTIONS

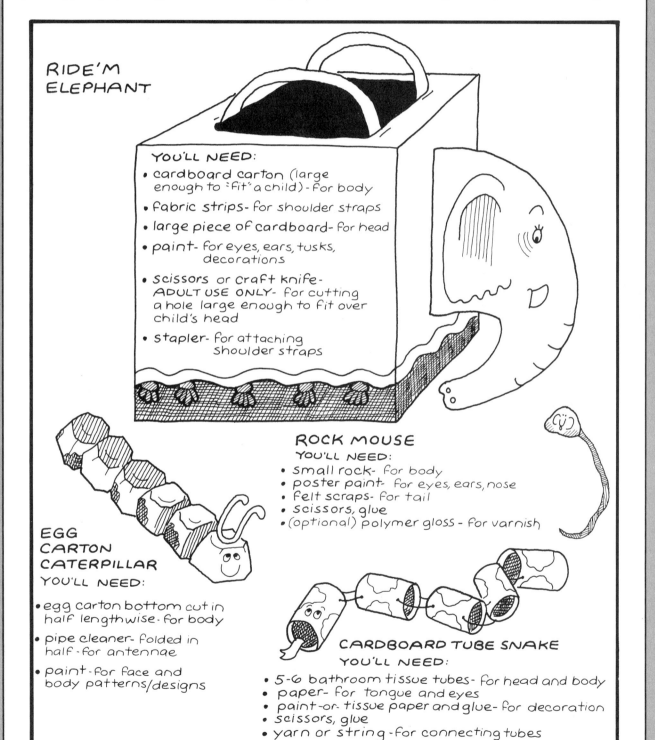

RIDE'M ELEPHANT

YOU'LL NEED:
- cardboard carton (large enough to "fit" a child) - for body
- fabric strips - for shoulder straps
- large piece of cardboard - for head
- paint - for eyes, ears, tusks, decorations
- scissors or craft knife - ADULT USE ONLY - for cutting a hole large enough to fit over child's head
- stapler - for attaching shoulder straps

ROCK MOUSE

YOU'LL NEED:
- small rock - for body
- poster paint - for eyes, ears, nose
- felt scraps - for tail
- scissors, glue
- (optional) polymer gloss - for varnish

EGG CARTON CATERPILLAR

YOU'LL NEED:
- egg carton bottom cut in half lengthwise - for body
- pipe cleaner - folded in half - for antennae
- paint - for face and body patterns/designs

CARDBOARD TUBE SNAKE

YOU'LL NEED:
- 5-6 bathroom tissue tubes - for head and body
- paper - for tongue and eyes
- paint - or - tissue paper and glue - for decoration
- scissors, glue
- yarn or string - for connecting tubes

what they eat. Take out your list of questions from home and see if together you can answer them. Let your child ask the zookeepers any questions you can not answer. Take pictures of your child's favorite animals.

Find a place to have your picnic, preferably near the playground. Relax, eat your lunch, and let your child get some exercise on the swings and slide.

In the afternoon, visit the "petting zoo." Here, your child can pet and feed lots of very friendly animals. By the afternoon, they will have had several hours of being fed by children, so they shouldn't be too aggressive. However, it's always a good idea to check their mood before you let your child enter the area.

If the zoo has a train, monorail, or bus, take a ride around the whole zoo. Your child can rediscover the experiences of the day and you can relax before the drive home.

In the evening or the next day, look through the photos you took at the zoo and the pictures your child cut out before the trip. He can paste the pictures on pieces of paper and draw backgrounds for each animal as he remembers them from his trip to the zoo. Then, he can dictate a story or some facts he has learned about the animal. You can staple or bind the pages together to make a zoo book for your child.

Over the next few days, continue to read zoo stories at bedtime. Your child will probably start talking about his next trip to the zoo as soon as he gets home. Kids and animals just go together!

More Trips and Follow Ups

Whenever you make special excursions with your child, try to build on the excitement and good feelings with some easy follow-up activities. These projects are not only fun but they help your child understand the experience better, while practicing his detail and recall skills at the same time.

Often, your child will be the one to initiate these follow-up activities. For example, after visiting the zoo, he may be eager to create his own zoo at home with his stuffed animals. Let him collect cardboard boxes of different sizes and shapes. You, then, can cut bars in the cardboard with a knife. Be sure to question him on how he plans to care for the animals in his zoo.

To a Movie

If your child really loves a movie, he will enjoy having something to remind him of it. Keep your ticket stubs and use them as the first item in a movie collage. Help your child find ads for the movie in local newspapers or photographs from it in magazines with movie reviews. Let him cut out or draw anything that reminds him of the plot or characters. An older child might enjoy making his own movie poster on a large piece of oaktag.

To a Play

If the play is a familiar one, like a fairy tale, your child may want to act it out himself when he gets home. Costumes are easy to make with old clothes and paper bags. (See page 103.)

He may enjoy putting on a puppet presentation with FINGER PUPPETS and a PAPER BAG THEATER. Make the finger puppets by rolling 1 1/2 to 2-inch square pieces of bendable cardboard into cylinders and taping them in place. Let your child decorate the puppets with markers, yarn, and fabric scraps. Then, cut a rectangle in the center of one side of a luncheon-sized paper bag to make a window. Have your child hold the paper bag with one hand and place his other hand with the puppets on his fingers in the bag so the puppets can be seen in the window. Showtime!

FINGER PUPPETS AND PAPER BAG STAGE

To a Concert

Children love to pretend they are leading an orchestra. The conductor is a very powerful person in the eyes of the young.

When you return from a concert, make a baton from an empty paper towel roll covered with foil. Put on a record and let your child conduct the Philharmonic.

To an Aquarium

It's great fun for the whole family to explore the ocean depths—especially on a hot summer's day.

When you return home, help your child make an easy PAPER BAG FISH. He can stuff newspaper into a brown lunch bag almost to the top; then tie the opening tightly with yarn. Let him fringe the remaining top part of the bag with scissors and cut an opening in the bottom of the bag for a mouth. He can use a marker or glue on paper eyes, fins, and other features he remembers from the fish he saw in the aquarium.

To a Farm

For many children today, farmers are named MacDonald and live in dells; cows jump over the moon. Farming today is quite mechanized; so children rarely have the opportunity to see firsthand what hard work farming once was and how much of the food we eat was tended and harvested by farmers. Recently, however, many historical farms and agricultural museums have opened around the country—there are over 200 in the United States today. At many of these farms, visitors are able to participate in farm activities, such as gathering eggs, milking cows, picking fruit, and churning butter. It is fascinating to young children to learn that butter comes from cows and that the orange juice that comes out of a can was once an orange on a tree.

When you get home from the farm, try making your own BUTTER. Help your child pour two cups of heavy cream into a plastic container. Add a marble. Cover tightly and shake. In about fifteen minutes—let your child shake the last five minutes or he will get bored—the BUTTER should separate from the thin white liquid—buttermilk. Press out all the liquid with a wooden spoon. Remove the marble. Let the butter chill and add a pinch of salt, if desired, before you spread it on bread or crackers.

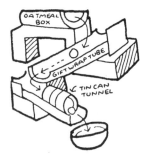

To an Amusement Park

As a follow up to your amusement park visit, help your child create his own "thrilling ride." Make ramps from cardboard tubes and round oatmeal boxes sliced in half. Tin cans without tops or bottoms can be tunnels if they do not have sharp edges. Prop the ramps on books, boxes, or chairs so that the ride can go from higher to lower levels. Have your child send ping-pong or golf balls through his ride.

FISH BOWL PICTURES

YOU'LL NEED:

chunks of paraffin wax

white paper

tape

paintbrush

blue food color- diluted with water

scissors

cotton tip stick

black paper

plastic kitchen wrap

WHAT TO DO:

1.
Draw fish shapes on white paper with paraffin wax chunks. (Shapes will be almost invisible.)

2.
Using a cotton tip stick or paintbrush, wash diluted food color over entire paper. Let dry thoroughly.

3.
Frame painting by cutting out a fish bowl shape in middle of black paper.

4.
On the back, tape down a piece of plastic kitchen wrap. From the front, the page will look like a glass fishbowl.

5.
Finally, tape fish painting to back of black paper so fish appear to be swimming in the "bowl."

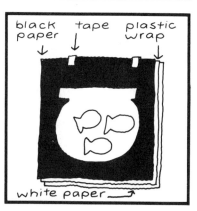

black paper   tape   plastic wrap

white paper

Museum Excursions

The illustrator of this book, Debby Dixler, is a museum educator as well as an artist and her insights coupled with her experiences with her five-year-old son, Scott, make her an invaluable resource on museums and young children. Many adults balk at the idea of taking a young child to a museum, but Debby and I have both found that with a little planning, a museum visit can be a terrific learning experience even for a preschooler.

Young children love collections, so the concept of a museum, a place which houses collections, is immediately intriguing to them. On returning from your first museum visit, your child may want to turn his room—perhaps your whole house—into a museum, much as Scott Dixler did. Scott lined up all of the shoes in his room for his "Shoe Collection;" then he found everything in the house that pertained to birds—toys, pictures, storybooks—for the "Bird Collection." His infant sister Hilary's room became the "Baby Room." His mother sat down and made labels for each item and collection with him and then Scott took his friends on "guided tours." This is a wonderful way for a young child to practice classification skills.

As I said in the beginning of this chapter, if you are lucky enough to have a museum nearby your home, it is better to take your child on several short trips there rather than an one daylong visit. Choose a theme for your visit; look at animals on one visit and save rocks for another time. This way, you can do a little reading with your child on the subject he is going to see and follow up with a project—going on a rock hunt—as soon as you get home to help him recall and extend what he learned.

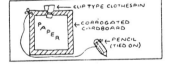

Try to find a Children's Museum in your area or a museum with a children's wing. In a Children's Museum, there are exhibits that your child can interact with. But, as long as you are there with your child answering questions and guiding his explorations, there are many kinds of museums your child will enjoy. You might want to make your child a simple clipboard to take along to the museum so that he can make sketches of what he sees. All you need is a piece of corrugated cardboard, a clip-style clothespin to hold the paper in place, and a pencil tied to the clothespin with a string.

Of course, dinosaur exhibits are the all-time favorites with young children. Science exhibits, in general, seem to spark their interest. One concept that perplexes many young children, whether they are looking at dinosaur skeletons or stuffed birds, is whether these animals are dead or alive. They want to know what the animal was like when it was alive, how it lived, what it ate, and so on.

Look at the animal environments at the museum. Then, encourage your child to try to replicate the bear environment he saw at the museum for his stuffed teddy at home. In the case of animals that are not extinct, it might be a good idea to follow up your museum trip with a visit to the zoo. You can point out living animals of the same family and talk about how they live.

If there is an art museum near your home, you might want to plan trips to see the painting and sculpture collections with your child. Looking at great works of art will help your child learn about colors and shapes. When you talk to him about the materials the artists used and their techniques, it will get your child's creative juices flowing.

Before your museum trip, get a few books out of the library that show beautiful paintings, sculptures, and other works of art. Your child will relate easily to the earliest art works—the cave paintings—and their childlike simplicity. At the other extreme, he will be fascinated by the works of modern artists like Jackson Pollock who experimented with vivid colors and unusual techniques, some of which, like spatter painting, your child can try himself.

On the way to the museum, ask your child this question, *"Why do you think people paint pictures?"* In a world where you can capture an image by pushing a button on a camera, this is a very interesting question. Tell him to think about this question as you view the pictures together. When you are looking at a painting, ask your child, *"Is the artist only painting what he sees? Can you tell me how he seems to be feeling?"* Talk about happy colors and angry ones and how different techniques make you feel different ways as you use them—watercolors are soothing; spatter painting can be playful or even angry, depending on the colors used.

When you return home from visiting a collection of paintings, let your child experiment with colors and media. Talk about the techniques used by great artists and encourage your child to try any that appeal to him.

▶ The French painter, Georges Seurat, used little dots of paint put close together to form large pictures. Your child can make dot pictures by using the erasers on new pencils as brushes and dipping them in poster paints. Pour the paint into styrofoam trays which have been covered by layers of paper towels so they act like stamp pads. Your child can either use white or yellow paint on dark blue or black construction paper or bright colors on light-colored paper.

▶ Vincent Van Gogh and other Expressionists loved working with bright colors and bold brush strokes. Your child might like to swirl on bright colors with his brush in a similar way to that shown in Van Gogh's "The Poppy Field" or any of his famous paintings of sunflowers.

▶ Piet Mondrian used bold shapes and lines and the colors black, white, and gray, and touches of red, blue, and yellow in his compositions. Show your child some of his paintings and then challenge him to paint a picture with lines and solid shapes, using only the colors preferred by Mondrian.

▶ Henri Matisse did some wonderful pictures with cut paper. Share these with your child and let him try some cutting and pasting.

▶ Let your child combine and glue pretty papers over paint in the style of Pablo Picasso or paste pictures from magazines over a painting as Max Ernst might have done.

Some day, you and your child may attend a special exhibit at a museum on a particular subject. After seeing many pictures of children, flowers, animals, or even portraits, your child may want to try his own interpretation of the subject. Encourage him to spend some time observing the real thing—go to a playground; visit a garden or a florist shop; spend some time at the zoo or at a pet store; look in the mirror before attempting a self-portrait.

Sculpture is another art form that young children can appreciate. Visit a sculpture garden with your child, if possible, one where he can touch the works of art or even climb on them. Before you go, you might play a game of "Statues" with your child—have him freeze in a postion when you give the signal. Let your child create his own sculptures with clay, play dough, wood scraps and glue, even crushed tin foil.

After your child has visited an art museum and created his own works of art, he may want to display them in his own art gallery. First, encourage him to choose his best works. Then, help him create mats—these can be store-bought—and frames, which can be made from Popsicle sticks, wood scraps, or cardboard. The pictures can be hung on a clothesline with clip style clothespins. Sculptures can be mounted on painted cardboard boxes or oatmeal containers. Choose a room for an exhibition or arrange a corner of your child's room for a permanent collection.

The works of art that your child observes in a museum are springboards for his own creations. Always remember that it is the processes that really intrigue young children and that there is no "right way" to be creative.

TOGETHER

MODERN ART MAKING

SQUEEZE BOTTLE PAINTING

YOU'LL NEED:

 empty plastic starch bottles

 poster paint

 clothespins

 large sheet of paper

 water

 old newspaper

 tape

WHAT TO DO:

1. Fill each plastic starch bottle with 1 color of poster paint which has been thinned with water so it squirts out easily.

2. Clothespin a large sheet of paper to a fence (or tape to a newspaper-covered wall). Have child stand back about 3' and squirt paint onto paper. It sprays, it drips, it blends colors!

SPATTER PAINTING
AND DRIP PAINTING

YOU'LL NEED:

 spoon

 old toothbrush

 large roll of paper

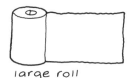 old newspaper

 poster paint

WHAT TO DO:

1. Roll out a long strip of paper on newspaper-covered floor.

2. Use toothbrush to spatter paint around paper. Child loads brush with paint, holds it out over paper and draws his thumb across bristles of the brush.

3. Have child dip spoon into paint and dribble paint across paper.

SUMMER

3

A Time for Growth

Independence Days

Summer Fantasy

Summer Relaxation

Summer Games Party

Choosing a Day Camp

A Time for Growth

Summer is a special time. There's just no way around it. The change in the weather brings changes in all areas of our lives—and, in most cases, in our dispositions, too. For one thing, summer means longer days—more time to get things done—and more time to relax. It's time to be outside—to play, explore, discover, and create. Even if you are working and/or your child is in a day camp or daycare program, longer days mean more special times for you and your child to spend together. Many of the projects and activities throughout this book, not just in this chapter, can easily be fitted into your summer plans.

For your child, summer is a time for growth—not only skills and concepts, but also emotional growth, growth towards independence. With more unstructured time in the summer, your child will have many opportunities to make decisions—choose activities or friends to play with—and take on responsibilities around the house—watering the flowers, washing her toys outside with soapy water, helping Daddy pick up sticks to start the barbecue. (Most likely, she had classroom chores at school and will miss the sense of accomplishment if there is nothing at home to take their place.)

Don't be surprised if your child is not too enthusiastic about her new opportunities and freedom at first. The structure and routines during the school year were like a security blanket for your child who is just developing her concepts of time and space. Her fears and tears back on the first day of school are the same ones she will experience on the first day of vacation. Until she feels comfortable with a new structure and new routines, she may very well feel lost—even in her own home.

One way to ease the transition from school to vacation is to maintain some of the old routines until they are replaced by new ones. Breakfast time, naptime, and bedtime routines can easily be worked into summer days. With this familiar framework to the day, your child will have a much easier time adjusting to more unstructured play periods and unfamiliar activities.

Also, it's a good idea to visit your child at school before the end of the year and observe the kinds of activities going on there, especially the ones your child particularly enjoys. With a little imagination, you can include some of these activities into your summer schedule at home. This will make it easier for your child not only to adjust to summer vacation, but also to the beginning of school in the fall.

If you have room, encourage your child to help you set up a special place with "school activities." Paper, crayons and markers, scissors, paste, play dough and/or clay, old magazines for cutting, favorite books, plastic numbers and letters, and other school-like supplies can go in this area. Plan with your child to do at least one activity daily here. This is also an excellent place to spend lots of time on a rainy day. Use the projects in this book and items brought home during the school year for inspiration. Let your child be the one to come up with the ideas and, if she remembers, to describe the process to you. Here are some additional ideas.

▶ This special corner is a good place for your child to record her summer adventures. Encourage her to "write" books about her summer activities, drawing or, if possible, taking photographs of special events. Let her dictate the text to you. These books will be fond memories for many summers to come and they can be shared at school in the fall.

▶ Children love receiving mail. Encourage your child to initiate an exchange of letters by writing or drawing pictures to send to a school friend or relative far away.

▶ Summertime is an excellent time for your child to start a collection— leaves, rocks, shells, postcards from vacations. There are ideas for storing and displaying the collection on pages 26 and 27.

▶ Help your child keep track of the summer weather. Put a daily calendar near a window with a thermometer outside. Help your child read and record the daily temperature and draw a picture to indicate weather conditions. Encourage her to listen to weather reports on TV or radio or read them to her out of the newspaper. Talk about how accurate the predictions are.

By letting your child take over many of the responsibilities for her play, you are also helping her develop thinking skills. *"How can I turn my swing set into a fort?"* or *"Where should I play if I want to stay cool?"* are interesting problems for her to solve. Let her help you figure out how to move inside activities out— water play, art projects, constructions. All of these take on a new dimension when you add fresh air. Let your child know in advance the limits of her play area outside and what she can and cannot do there. Point out dangerous plants or places where she might get hurt. You might even make small signs reminding her of dangerous places. As always, your child needs a secure framework in which to practice her independence.

That extra summer time also provides your child the chance to reflect on what she has done and evaluate whether it worked or not. Take time at the end of the day to talk over the games she especially liked and/or the things that didn't turn out as she planned them, so that you can help her plan for the next day. Not only is she practicing her thinking skills, but she also is having a special sharing experience with you.

Independence Days

Summer is a time to relax—but only after you have accomplished all of the things you have to do in a day. To get work done around the house with your child home from school takes some creative planning on your part, but it can be fun and full of learning possibilities for your child. The key is to keep some independent activities handy to amuse your child when you are busy.

Children love dress up. If you have a box of dress-up clothes, fabric scraps, artificial flowers, and old costume jewelry in the closet, you can encourage your child to play with them as you take care of your chores. Also, you might want to check out the creative ideas in <u>Easy Costumes You Don't Have to Sew</u> by Goldie Taut Chernoff. The trick here is to make these dress-up clothes special. Don't bring them out too often or they will lose their allure. The box of costume jewelry can become pirate treasure to be buried in the backyard or sandbox—when you need some time and space.

Your child may be the practical type and prefer a real job to fantasy play. Let her shine Daddy's shoes. Keep a shoebox with your child's name on it in the closet near the shoes. Place an old shirt or smock in it with a few pieces of newspaper, rags, and polish. Show your child how to take the laces out of the shoes to be polished, how to spread the polish with a rag, how to use a buffing cloth, and finally, how to replace all the equipment in the box. With very young shoeshine kids, keep some worn-out shoes around for practice.

TOGETHER

Let your child help you prepare these Easy Picnics. Then, enjoy them together.

For those times when you need a few minutes to talk on the phone, concentrate on a problem, or just relax, keep junk mail (unopened) in a special basket for your child. Let your child open them, cut out any available coupons, and use the colorful ads for collages.

If you're working outside or your child is allowed outside alone, there are many independent activities she can do.

▶ .Let her paint the outside of the house—with water. Give her a bucket with some water in it and a paintbrush. Have the hose handy, if she runs out of "paint." Water does change the color of most surfaces temporarily, so she will feel like she is really painting.

▶ Give your child some colored chalk and let her decorate the cement porch or the sidewalk. Children love to create huge murals or stories or just to write their names in large colorful letters. It's a welcome change from pencil and paper. A summer shower or the garden hose washes away the chalk.

▶ Water or sand play in a plastic tub will keep your child occupied for hours. If you save empty plastic containers, you don't even need to buy toys for her to play with. A most resourceful idea for a water/sand toy comes from preschool teacher Susan Coons. She suggests that you take a clean gallon-size bleach container and cut it in half horizontally just below the handle. You now have a funnel or scoop and a bucket. With your child, add a rope handle to the bucket and some permanent marker drawings for decoration and your child will have some very original play utensils.

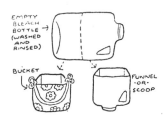

EMPTY BLEACH BOTTLE → (WASHED AND RINSED)

BUCKET

FUNNEL ·OR· SCOOP

EASY PICNIC MENUS

1. FAVORITE JOBS- CUTTING, SLICING, CHOPPING

cottage cheese

fresh fruit salad

2. FINGER FOODS

sliced apples

popcorn

sliced cheese

3. FUN TO MAKE AND DECORATE

carrot chips

raisins

celery sticks

rice cake

peanut butter

fresh vegetables

shredded carrots

raisin

ANIMAL SANDWICH- make your favorite sandwich filling. Prepare sandwich and use cookie cutters to make shapes.

Summer Fantasy

If you're not planning a vacation away from home this summer, try one in your own backyard. You and your child can travel to the far ends of the earth--the desert, the ocean, a mountaintop, or a jungle. Your destination can be as far away as your imagination allows you to go.

Not only will you have fun on your trip, you will also be giving your child valuable practice in using her imagination. Through this kind of play, she will have the opportunity to express her feelings, fantasies, dreams, and creative thoughts. Fantasy play is an important avenue to learning for your child. She uses role-playing to make sense of all that she sees, hears, smells, tastes, and feels in her life; and it also helps clarify things beyond her senses that she imagines.

TOGETHER

Make some fantastic ice creations together with Ice Cube Fun. Anything cold is appreciated on a sultry summer day. Any mess you make is easier to clean.

One way that you can show that you approve of her fantasy play is to participate yourself. Start planning your shared adventure by reading some books like On Vacation by Richard Scarry and What Ernie and Bert Did on Their Summer Vacation by Patricia Thackray. Encourage your child to pick a place she would like to visit.

Head for the Sahara Desert or Death Valley in your backyard sandbox. Introduce the adventure by reading a book like Let's Play Desert by Inger and Lasse Sandberg or the Time-Life book The Desert. (Others in this series include The Forest, The Sea, and The Mountains.) A buried butter tub filled with water becomes an oasis for small plastic animals. The same sandbox or a dirt pile can become a mountain or even a volcano with a little imagination. You can make your volcano come alive by burying an empty can in the mountain and filling it with a 1/4 cup of baking soda. "Lava" will come pouring out of the mouth of the can when you add vinegar. If you bury pennies or chicken bones in the sand or dirt, your child can dig for them and be an archaeologist or even a pirate.

"LAVA":
MAGIC
SOLUTION
+
BAKING
SODA

The sandbox becomes the seashore when you bury some shells for your child to find. Read the book A Day at the Beach by Mircea Vasilui. After some time at the seashore, you can become deep-sea divers and explore the ocean floor—a wading pool. Hide a treasure chest—a traveler's soap dish—at the bottom of the sea and don't forget to leave a little treasure inside. This game is terrific for the child who is not yet comfortable getting her face wet—a swimming prerequisite. Your wading pool could also be a training ground for the next Olympics.

Take another wet adventure and visit Niagara Falls by propping the garden hose on some bricks or flower pots and surrounding it with plants. Let the water cascade into a tub, large bowl, or pan which becomes a lake on which to sail miniature boats.

Surround the tub with lots of different plants, add some plastic animals, and you're ready for an African safari. Read Annie and the Wild Animals by Jan

ICE CUBE FUN

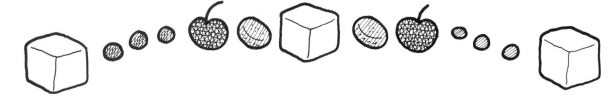

ICE CUPS

juice

ice↑

Fill paper cups almost full with water. Freeze 1- 1½ hours or until cup is frozen all around edges. Break open the top. Drain out water. Remove from paper cup. Fill with juice and use immediately.

FANCY ICE CUBES

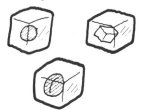

Freeze water in ice cube trays. Add a cherry, peach slice, strawberry slice, pineapple chunk, or blueberry to each cube before it freezes.

ICE BLOCKS

Boil and cool about ½ gallon of water. (Boiling water freezes clear.) Pour water into a paper ½ gallon milk carton about ½ full. Freeze until almost firm. Remove from freezer and place roses, lillies, mint sprigs, etc. into partially frozen ice. Return to freezer until frozen solid. Peel away carton to use.

Brett and Margaret Lane's excellent books <u>The Lion,</u> <u>The Giraffe,</u> and <u>The Elephant</u> to help your child get into the mood.

Take a look around your backyard and you'll come up with more ideas.

▶   A grassy area can become a forest, a jungle, or even a fairyland—check for elves on your toadstools!

▶   Swings can be jets or rocket ships that will take your child to new planets. Or, she can be a circus performer on a trapeze.

▶   The top of the jungle gym can become the top of a mountain, or a forest ranger's lookout, or the crow's nest of a pirate ship.

It's fun to combine areas and have your pirate ship sail in your pool and then land in the sandbox to hunt for buried treasure. Encourage your child to use her imagination and go on lots of backyard adventures. Research shows that children who play make-believe games tend to be less aggressive, are less demanding of adult attention, and develop better language skills. What more can you ask?

TOGETHER

Create this simple Butterfly Fan with your child. The shape can vary.

BUTTERFLY FAN

YOU'LL NEED:

 tape

1 craft (or popsicle stick)

 scissors

 crayons

felt tip markers

WHAT TO DO:

1 Cut a butterfly shape from a paper plate.

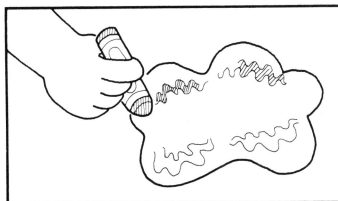

2 Decorate butterfly shape

Butterfly Fan

3 Using tape, attach butterfly to craft stick.

Summer Relaxation

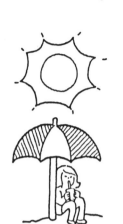

No one has to show me how or when to relax in the summer—it comes very naturally, but, sometimes, a young child will need a little help to wind down and just enjoy the season from a quiet space. Especially during the hot hours after lunch, when your child is drowsy, but not in the mood for a nap, a few calm, soothing activities can come in handy.

Certain materials lend themselves to relaxing activities. As "yucky" as it sounds, mud is just such a medium on a hot summer day. Let your child add water to clean soil to make the mud. She can feel the lovely squishiness with her hands and even her toes. She can "paint" with it on cement or make structures by packing it in tin containers. <u>Mudpies and Other Recipes</u> by Marjorie Winslow is a resource you and your child will both enjoy.

Any water play is relaxing and blowing bubbles is especially so because everything seems to happen in slow motion. You can make your own bubble solution by mixing 1/4 cup of liquid detergent, 1/4 cup of glycerin, and 2 cups of water. Store in one large or several small jars. Make a homemade bubble pipe by poking a hole in the side of a styrofoam cup, halfway between the top and the bottom. Insert a straw in the hole so that it goes about halfway into the cup. Put the solution in a pan and let your child dip the rim of the cup into it. Then, she can blow gently on the straw and jiggle the bubble free when it forms. Talk about the beautiful rainbow colors on the bubble. Have your child pretend she is a bubble floating in the air.

The key to the success of relaxing activities is YOU. If you are relaxed, your child will calm down much more easily. Slow movements and a quiet voice will set the stage. Try the following activities with your child. See who falls into a peaceful sleep first.

▶ Lie down on the grass. Close your eyes. Listen to the sounds of summer. Ask your child if she can hear birds singing, insects buzzing, a tree moving in the breeze, a leaf rustling. Encourage her to listen for an airplane overhead, voices in the distance, a car passing in the street. You might want to tape some of these sounds one day and have your child try to identify them later.

▶ Now, open your eyes. Be sure to warn your child NOT to look directly at the sun. Together look up at the clouds and see if you can see them moving. Can your child find objects or animals in the clouds? Look for the moon in daytime sky. Try to observe insects flying. Find a tree. Watch the leaves and the branches move.

▶ Take your child on an imaginary trip after both of you close your eyes. Choose a place that your child really enjoys visiting. Describe it in great detail. Talk about being there. Your child will pick up on the imagery and begin to talk about it, herself. This is a perfect activity to do just before she falls asleep.

TOGETHER

Fans can create relaxing, cool breezes. This one is a challenge to make.

Try to spend some relaxed time together with your child on a regular basis in the summer. It's really special!

POPSICLE STICK FAN

YOU'LL NEED:

1 brass paper fastener   glue   scissors   6" x 12" piece of paper   4 craft (or popsicle sticks)   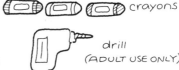 crayons   drill (ADULT USE ONLY)

WHAT TO DO:

 1. Fold paper in half.

 2. Cut a quarter circle (as shown):

3" ←FOLD
←FOLD
3" ←FOLD

 3. Fold paper in half and in half again. Open it up.

FOLD → FOLD

 4. Accordian-fold the paper so that each crease already made alternates forward and backward.

 5. With a small bit, adult drills a hole in bottom of each craft stick.

 6. Attach craft sticks together with a paper fastener.

 7. Decorate fan paper and glue to sticks.

BACK OF FAN

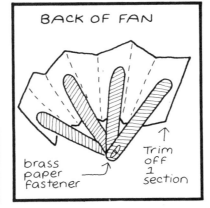

brass paper fastener

Trim off 1 section

FRONT OF FAN

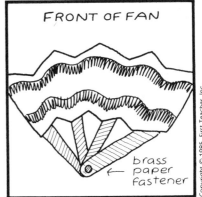

brass paper fastener

Summer Games Party

Summer is the time for family get-togethers, block parties, fairs, and just being outdoors with friends. Why not plan a party everyone–from two to eighty-two–will enjoy. Instead of taking everyone to a local carnival, have one at home! Set up special areas of your yard or a blocked-off street for booths for each event. Booths are no more elaborate than tables, large cardboard cartons, or just a roped-off area. Here are some ideas for easy games of skill.

▶ Let children throw a frisbee through an 18"-diameter circle cut into a sheet that has been hung on a clothesline.

▶ Tape or glue two styrofoam cups together, bottom to bottom. Contestants try to toss a marshmallow in the top cup up in the air and then catch it in the bottom cup.

▶ Have children pitch pennies into a row of shallow bowls.

▶ For a magnet fishing game, tie a string to a stick and attach a magnet to the hanging end of the string. Make tissue paper fish–your child can help you–and attach a paper clip to each. Let the children go fishing.

▶ Poke about 16 wooden clothespins into a cardboard carton, with four in each row, to make a ring toss game. Let your young friends toss rubber jar rings.

▶ Older children and adults will have fun with a ping-pong ball and a plastic flexible straw. Bend the straw upwards. Put the longer end in your mouth and blow a steady stream of air. Place the ping-pong ball on the straw and see who can keep it in the air the longest.

Don't forget large group games like:
■ Egg-in-the-spoon race
■ Pillow case race
■ Backward race

Make sure that all the children at your homemade fair win some kind of prize. Have a big barbecue to end the festivities.

TOGETHER

Make homemade Ice Cream to cool off from all the games.

ICE CREAM

YOU'LL NEED:

 1 envelope unflavored gelatin

8" baking pan

3/4 cup hot milk - heated to boiling

1/4 cup cold milk

spoon

3 cups fruit - strawberries, blueberries, peaches

2 cups heavy cream - whipped

1/4 tsp. vanilla extract

3/4 cup sugar

blender

bowl

WHAT TO DO:

1. In a blender, sprinkle gelatin over cold milk. Let stand 4 minutes.

2. Add hot milk and process in blender about 2 minutes.

3. Gradually, add fruit, sugar, and vanilla. Process until smooth.

4. Pour into bowl and chill, stirring occasionally until mixture mounds slightly when dropped from spoon.

5. Fold chilled gelatin mixture into the whipped cream.

6. Pour into 8" baking pan. Freeze until firm.

Choosing a Day Camp

The day camp experience is a wonderful one for many young children and a viable alternative to babysitters or daycare centers for working parents. Dr. Margery A. Kranyik, noted Early Childhood educator, provided the guidelines which I have used to choose a camp for my daughter.

To find a day camp, look into programs offered by your local YMCA, YWCA, YM/WHA, church organizations, or boy's or girl's clubs. Nursery schools in your area may offer day camps as an informal follow-up to their school year programs, too.

Don't sign up for the first camp that you see. Look at several, if possible. Summer is a fun time for your child and she should be active--and outdoors-- as much as possible. Try to find a camp that offers swimming instruction, arts and crafts, nature studies, field trips in the community, noncompetitive sports, and a quiet storytime each day.

The following checklist of Dr. Kranyik's will help you decide if a day camp is suitable for your child.

▶ **DIRECTOR AND STAFF**
1. Does the administration and staff have experience working with young children?
2. What is the ratio of counselors to campers?
3. Are the swimming instructors certified?

▶ **GOALS**
1. Will the camp encourage your child's individual hobbies and interests?
2. Are the groups coeducational?
3. Are parents invited to visit and contribute in some way?

▶ **PROGRAM**
1. Is transportation provided?
2. What type of swimming instruction is available?
3. What provisions are made for naps or rest time?
4. Are meals and snacks provided?
5. What is the daily schedule?
6. Is the schedule structured or informal?
7. What happens if it rains?
8. What personal belongings are needed daily--athletic shoes, snack, swimsuit, jacket or sweater, pillow or something to rest on?

▶ **MEDICAL CARE**
1. Are there trained medical personnel on the camp premises at all times?
2. Is there a doctor on call for emergencies?
3. What type of medical release form must a parent sign?
4. What provisions are made for a child who becomes ill during the day?
5. Is there an infirmary for isolation from the group?

▶ FEES AND EXPENSES

1. What does the fee include?
2. Do the children need spending money everyday?
3. Is there a discount rate for several children in a family?
4. Is there a rebate policy if your child has to leave the camp session early due to an emergency or illness?
5. Does the camp have comprehensive liability insurance?

A good camp director should be able to answer all of these questions for you. The information will give you a picture of life at a particular camp, but, also try to visit the camp before you decide. At least, talk to other families who have attended the camp before.

Once you have chosen a camp--your child's input is an important plus--talk about the whole experience enthusiastically. Remember that even though your child may have been in nursery school or a daycare center, day camp will be a new experience, and hence new anxieties. Be sure that your child always knows where you will be when she is at camp--and don't make your plans sound more fun than hers. Let her bring something special from home until she gets adjusted.

Go shopping together for clothes or equipment she may need. Even if the camp has a uniform, she can be responsible for choosing her sneakers.

On the first day of camp, be especially enthusiastic. You may be having separation problems yourself, but just remember that this experience is all part of growing up. You need not--in fact, you should not--spend all of your special times together. Then, your child would have nothing new and exciting to share with you just before she goes to sleep!

VACATIONS 4

Going Away

Transportation

Pack Up Your Routines

In a Tent

By the Sea

On the Slopes

Going Away

To a young child, vacations can mean fun and excitement–or separation and anxiety. Vacations usually mean new experiences and this means a change from the secure, familiar environment in which your child feels safe. In some instances, vacations mean that Mommy and Daddy are going away from home, and, in others, the whole family is going away. But, no matter what the circumstance, vacations bring to your child's mind some kind of separation.

Until they reach a certain stage of development, babies have terrible separation anxieties when you leave their sight. Your child may not become frightened when you leave the room, but until he develops the pattern in his mind that when you go away, you always come back, he will begin to worry after only a short time away from you. The security of your child's world is shaken even when you take off for a short weekend's rest.

This chapter is mainly about family vacations, but there are things that you can do when you, ALONE, are taking a vacation to make the experience a positive one for your child. Parenting expert and daycare director, Sherry Burrell, has some excellent suggestions to ease the pain of separation.

► Try not to involve your child in your plans before it is necessary. When the suitcases come out or when you sense that your child needs to know what is going on, explain that you are going away and coming back soon.

► Use a calendar to help your child understand the time involved in the vacation. Circle the day you will leave and the day you are returning and let your child keep the calendar with him, so that he can mark off the days. Include some special events for your child on the calendar while you are away–a trip to the zoo, play dates, a Saturday movie matinee–things for him to look forward to every few days.

► Encourage your child to act out parts of the upcoming separation with toys as props. Have the family get into the car, drive to the airport, and have Mommy and Daddy get on a toy airplane, which then takes off and flies away. Have a doll representing your child going to Grandma's house (a dollhouse) or wherever he will be staying while you are gone. Be sure to conclude your play with your return and everything going back to normal.

► Give your child an envelope filled with the latest family photographs for him to keep while you are away.

► Be sure that whoever is caring for your child while you are away knows his routines and understands the importance of maintaining them as much as possible. Familiar bedtime stories, favorite foods, basic rules, and daily schedules all make your child feel more comfortable and secure. Of course, make sure that your child's favorite toy, blanket, pillow, and stuffed animal stay with him wherever he goes while you are away.

► While you are gone, be sure to send lots of postcards and perhaps leave little treats for your child to receive ESPECIALLY FROM YOU at different times. *"Your Mommy thought you would like this grown-up headband like Daddy's to wear to gym class today."* If it is possible, you may want to call·

your child to keep in touch. Don't be disappointed if your child is not overjoyed to talk with you. My daughter often refuses to talk with me when I am away; it is her way of saying she is angry with me for leaving. No matter what you do, no matter how much fun your child has while you are gone, he will be a little hurt and angry that you left him. After all, he's only human.

Before a Family Vacation

Many of the activities suggested above can also apply to family vacations. Even if your child is going along on the vacation, he is still leaving home, friends, and his everyday routines. He needs your support to make the transition and enjoy the new experiences. Here are some additional ideas.

▶ Starting about a week before you leave, focus some activities on the upcoming vacation. Read books about the places you are going or the method of transportation you will be using; show photographs of the areas you will be visiting; experiment with unusual foods you may be trying at your destination; help your child cut and paste pictures from magazines to make beach or skiing collages.

▶ Look at maps or map puzzles with your child. Show him where he lives and where you are going. Even three-year-olds like to see where they are on a map and where they are going for their vacation. Take a map with you as you travel. Young children like to see how much further they must travel to reach a destination, too.

▶ If you are planning to visit relatives or old friends, show your child pictures of the people in question and explain your relationship to them. You might want to let your child speak with them on the phone before you leave. Encourage him to ask them questions about what he will be doing and where he will be staying on your trip.

▶ Have your child help you pack his suitcase. Give him some choices about what he would like to bring—keeping in mind that once you give him the choice, whatever he chooses goes in the suitcase.

When you are planning a trip, remember that at each stage of development, your child has different travel needs. The cartoon should help you understand some of his needs.

TRAVELS WITH 2 YEAR OLDS

The 2 year old is easily over-excited by long days and much activity. The 2 year old needs time for physical activity and rest.

For the 2 year old, a visit to the shoe store, nearby park, or mailbox are ideal trips.

TRAVELS WITH 4 + 5 YEAR OLDS

Play and language continue to play an important role in helping 4 and 5 year olds understand a trip.

I'll be the ticket-taker and you be the engineer!

THIS SIDE UP

TRAVELS WITH 3 YEAR OLDS

The 3 year old still needs his cuddly animal and many reassurances about new noises and experiences. The 3 year old can begin to look forward to the trip through play and language.

Transportation

When you are preparing to travel with your child, be sure to prepare him for the type of transportation he will use as well as his destination. In her book, <u>The Magic Years</u>, Selma Fraiberg describes a preschool boy who was told that he and his family were taking a plane trip to Europe. On the day of their departure, his parents found him crying. He explained his problem this way, *"Today is the day we are going to fly to Europe and I still don't know how to fly."*

Be sensitive to your child's thoughts and fantasies about the trip as well as the reality of the situation. As soon as you know the mode of transportation, go the library with your child and bring home some simple books on the subject. <u>Cars and Trucks and Things That Go</u> by Richard Scarry not only describes a fun family car trip, but will also take your child to an airport and a train station. It is a favorite of my family and will keep your child occupied on the trip as well as before it.

If you can, it's always a good idea to take a "dry run" and visit an airport, railroad station, or pier. When he sees the train, plane, or boat up close, you will have a chance to deal with any questions or fears he might have in advance of the trip. If he meets someone else arriving or leaving, he will feel more comfortable about his own travel adventure.

At the airport, show your child the metal detectors, the baggage claim area, control tower, conveyor belts loading luggage, baggage carts and trucks and identify all of the people in uniform. This will save your child a lot of confusion and probably anxiety the actual day he is traveling. The most important thing is to prepare your child for the size of the planes and the loud noises they make. When you get home from the airport, you may want to let your child be the pilot in a large carton and "fly" you off on a vacation.

Whatever way you travel, make sure you bring along enough toys, books, and snacks to keep your child occupied. On the positive side, remember that everything fascinates young children--how they get there just as much as their destination.

In the Car

TOGETHER

Make the take-along Snack Server for long trips. Your child will enjoy choosing his snacks.

Because your child will want to explore everything he sees, hears, tastes, touches, and smells, it's a good idea to plan a leisurely car trip, if it is to be a long one. When you are planning your route, look through AAA travel books, pamphlets, and other guidebooks to find out about places you can stop along the way like museums, zoos, and theme parks. Watch for billboards advertising local attractions like fairs and circuses. Also, be on the lookout for the many inexpensive or often free, unstructured attractions that will entertain your child just as well as a festival or rodeo. These include farms, "pick-your-own" orchards, roadside stands, playgrounds, lookout points on highways, beaches, and piers. In places like these, your child should feel comfortable to explore freely and you can relax and stretch your legs, too.

SNACK SERVER

YOU'LL NEED:

plastic
foam egg cartons

plastic
knife

assorted snack foods
(see drawing below)

WHAT TO DO:

1.
Wash and dry egg carton carefully.

2.
Cut each food into small pieces so that several will fit into an egg carton section. Child can help cut foods if he uses a plastic knife.

3.
Set out the foods on a table and let child pick his own snacks and place items into egg carton sections.

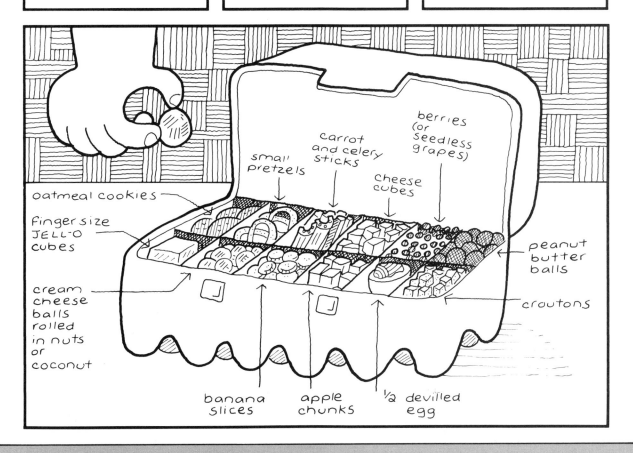

oatmeal cookies

finger size JELL-O cubes

cream cheese balls rolled in nuts or coconut

small pretzels

carrot and celery sticks

berries (or seedless grapes)

cheese cubes

peanut butter balls

croutons

banana slices

apple chunks

½ devilled egg

Provide a box for collecting found treasures, some paper and crayons for making texture rubbings, and a ball for just having fun. You might also bring along a homemade clipboard (see page 60) with some paper for your child to make tallies on the road of cars, license plates, familiar food chain outlets, gas station logos, or just to draw whatever intrigues him.

Spend some time explaining the meaning of road signs to your child. Tell him the meaning of the solid and dotted lines on the road. On an uninteresting stretch of road, challenge your child to tell you when you can pass other cars and when you can't. Don't forget to point out and discuss bridges, tunnels, mountains, valleys, rivers, interesting buildings and motor vehicles, and other sights along the way. Your child's vocabulary really increases when you talk your way through a trip and the time passes much more quickly.

TOGETHER

Make Crazy Cars with your child. They're easy to pack and take on a vacation.

Give your child a road map so that he can follow the progress of your trip. Outline the route with a bright-colored marker. Whenever you stop, mark your progress with another pen.

Play games in the car like "Close your Eyes and Tell Me What You Hear." If the surrounding noises aren't very interesting, turn on the radio and try to guess the name of a song after only hearing a few seconds of it. Or, before you turn it on, have everyone guess what you will hear--a song, a commercial, the announcer's voice. Change stations, guessing before you do so.

Tell stories and play word games in the car. Have everyone tell part of a story and interact with the passing environment as they tell it. *"Once there was a little boy and he lived in a house like that one."* (Point to house.) *"He had two dogs like those."* (Point out the window.) *"His dad worked at an ice cream parlor..."*

On a Train
Read some books about trains before your trip. Freight Train by Donald Crew and The Little Engine That Could by Watty Piper are two good choices that also will demonstrate to your child the difference between fiction and nonfiction books.

Before you board, show your child the engine. Be sure to point out the restrooms, dining car, parlor car, and any other interesting attractions inside the train.

Many of the same games that are played in a car can be played on a train trip. On your trip, you may pass other trains. Point out the different types of cars, especially on a freight train. Encourage him to see how many different logos--there may be several different companies' cars on one train since they are interchangable--he can find on a passing freight train. Teach your child train songs like "I've Been Working on the Railroad," and "Casey Jones."

CRAZY CARS

YOU'LL NEED:

walnut shell halves

paper scraps

marbles

scissors

glue

paper towel tubes

cardboard box top

WHAT TO DO:

1. Cut out paper scraps for wheels, windshield, and lights. Glue onto walnut shell.

marble

2. Place marble under shell.

3. Place a few CRAZY CARS in a box and tilt box to watch 'em go!

4. Use paper towel tubes, boxes, and chairs to make downhill ramps.

5. Put CRAZY CARS on top of ramps and let them race to the bottom.

TOGETHER

Pack Up Your Routines

Wherever you go on your vacation–hotel, resort, campsite–it's important to bring along a little bit of home whenever you travel with a young child. Children adapt so much better to being away from home and their normal schedule, if you include some short, consistent routines within the many new experiences. These routines make your child feel secure and better able to go along with the constant daily changes that vacations bring. There are three daily routines that seem to "travel well" : wake up, meals, and bedtime.

Even at home, it is important for your child to have an early morning routine. On weekdays, everyone may be in a rush, but your child still will appreciate knowing what's coming–wake up, breakfast, brush teeth, get dressed, off to school, or whatever. On weekends, this pattern may vary a little, perhaps including a family cuddle-in-bed session. If your child is an early riser (earlier than you), you probably have an established routine for what he is to do until you wake up–reading, watching TV, playing quietly with toys. Bring these routines–the weekend ones–with you on your vacation and your child will be able to start the day off confident and relaxed.

Family mealtimes can be stressful even at home. When you travel, the problems multiply whether you are in restaurants, strange kitchens, or hotel dining rooms. Try to eat at the same times you do at home, if possible. This may be the only routine part of the meal. If you are doing the cooking, short, simple meals with a minimum of preparation seem to work best. If you go to a restaurant, choose one where the whole family will be welcome. Have some little toys or paper and crayons to entertain your child in between courses. In foreign countries, try to find simple foods–most places serve grilled chicken and have some kind of bread. If your child is a very picky eater, you may want to bring along a jar of peanut butter, just to be safe.

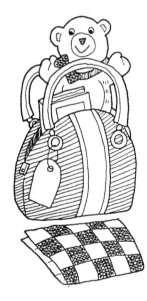

Bedtimes are critical on vacations. A well-rested child is much better able to cope with new people, places, and experiences. Before you leave, observe the "props" your child uses to feel safe and comfortable at night–a blanket, pillow, stuffed animal, pajamas, favorite book. Pack as many of these as space will allow. Don't burden yourself with quilts, large pillows, or ten pound books. Then, perform as much of your child's bedtime ritual as your travel schedule will allow. You might throw in a backrub, even if it isn't part of your normal routine, to help make up for the unfamiliar setting.

If you are used to telling bedtime stories instead of reading them, try to recount the past day's events for your child, putting them in story form. This isn't a time to quiz your child about what happened all day, rather it is an opportunity for both of you to review the fun you had together.

These are just a few examples of the routines you may want to include when traveling with your child. You know which rituals are truly important to your child. The idea is to make a hotel, cruise ship, trailer, dude ranch–wherever you go–feel like home.

In a Tent

Camping trips make wonderful vacations for the whole family. On your first time out, two days and one night are enough time to create an exciting adventure for a young child.

Do some research on campgrounds beforehand. Talk to friends, stores that sell camping equipment, and guides to local facilities to find the right place to go. Choose a place that has campsites handy to parking facilities, water, bathrooms, and fireplaces. If you are able to choose between a few equally good campsites, describe or even visit the alternatives with your child and let him help you choose.

Become familiar with your equipment before you leave home. In fact, you may want to have a backyard campout before you venture out into the woods. Set up your tent in the yard and let your child play in it before the trip. This also allows you to familiarize yourself with the set-up procedures and gives you the opportunity to check a new tent for holes or other damage.

Let your child help you with planning and gathering supplies. Learn about camping together using the Boy Scout Handbook or nature guides as resources. Make a list of supplies together and assign your child to check them off as they are packed. Have him help you decide what food you'll need and take him along to buy it.

It's as important for your child to bring "a little bit of home" with him on a camping trip as it is on a trip to a hotel or resort. Encourage him to pack his favorite small blanket, book—Mercer Mayer's Just Me and My Dad is a hilarious camping adventure—stuffed animal, or doll in his backpack or even a laundry bag which he can carry.

Also, bring along some of his usual routines. Bathtime may be an outdoor shower, your meals will certainly be out-of-the-ordinary, but going to bed and wake-up times should be somewhat consistent with your child's normal routine. Remember that going to bed in a strange place with the strange feel of the sleeping bag, and the very strange sounds of the night can be scary for a young child. Take a nighttime walk before your child goes to bed and identify as many of the sounds as you can. Also, show him that there are no wild animals or monsters lurking in the woods to disturb his sleep. Plan to be around if he should wake up in the middle of the night.

Let your child help you with setting up the tent, gathering firewood, blowing up the air mattresses, preparing the food, cleaning up your campsite, and any other chores he can manage. The work is all part of the camping experience. When you are done with the chores, it's fun to relax together, take walks in the woods, swim in the pond or stream, or just sit back and enjoy nature.

TOGETHER

Let your child help you prepare these unusual Camp-out Recipes on the next two pages. They are also fun for backyard cookouts.

CAMP-OUT RECIPES

PAN PIZZA

YOU'LL NEED:

- frozen bread dough or hot roll mix
- 2 Tblsp. oil
- shredded mozzarella cheese or muenster cheese
- tomato sauce
- covered skillet
- spatula

WHAT TO DO:

1. Spread oil in skillet bottom.
2. Spread dough over entire bottom.
3. Cover tightly and cook slowly over coals about 6-8 minutes.
4. Turn over dough with a spatula.
5. Add sauce over dough.
6. Sprinkle with cheese.
7. Cover and continue baking until crust is baked and cheese is melted.

TWIG TOAST

YOU'LL NEED:

- 1 slice bread
- 1 twig with forked end ☆

☆ DO NOT use a cherry tree twig.

WHAT TO DO:

1. Adult whittles twig to sharp points.
2. Stick bread onto forked twig.
3. Hold over fire to toast.

S'MORES

Toast a marshmallow on a stick and then place it between 2 graham crackers with a piece of a chocolate bar.

CORN-ON-THE-COB

YOU'LL NEED:

- 1 ear of corn
- 1 Tblsp butter
- 1 ice cube or 2 Tblsp. water
- aluminum foil

WHAT TO DO:

1. Put 1 ear of corn on a piece of aluminum foil.
2. Add 1 Tblsp. butter and 1 ice cube (or 2 Tblsp. water).
3. Wrap up foil. Secure tightly and twist ends.
4. Roast in coals or on a grill 10-15 minutes. Turn frequently.

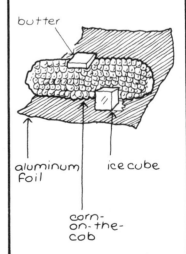

butter

aluminum foil

ice cube

corn-on-the-cob

BAKED FRUIT DESSERTS

YOU'LL NEED:

- 1 apple
- 1 banana
- 2 Tblsp. mini-marshmallows
- 2 Tblsp. chocolate chips
- dash of cinnamon or whole cinnamon stick
- aluminum foil
- plastic knife
- apple corer

cinnamon stick

aluminum foil

WHAT TO DO:

1. Core apple. Sprinkle on cinnamon or force cinnamon stick through apple. Wrap in foil.

2. Cut a wedge of banana open, leaving peel intact. Stuff with mini-marshmallows and chocolate chips. Cover with cut peel. Wrap in foil.

3. Place near coals or on a grill. Cook banana until stuffing is melted. Cook apple until soft.

BOIL-IN-A-BAG CUSTARD

YOU'LL NEED:

- 1 egg
- 3/4 cup milk
- 2 tsp. sugar
- dash of vanilla
- dash of cinnamon
- ziplocking bag
- deep pan of boiling water

WHAT TO DO:

1. Put all ingredients into zip locking bag. "Zip" closed.

2. Adult places bag in deep pan of boiling water.

3. Cook 6-10 minutes.

4. Adult removes bag from water.

5. Eat custard from bag or pour immediately into a bowl.

DUMP SHORTCAKE

YOU'LL NEED:

- 1 lb can of fruit cocktail or chunky fruits
- 2 cups biscuit mix
- 1/3 cup dry milk
- 1/4 cup sugar
- 1/3 cup water
- 1 egg
- zip locking bag
- covered skillet
- spatula
- OPTIONAL: cream

WHAT TO DO:

1. Dump can of fruit cocktail or chunky fruits into a heavy metal skillet

2. Mix biscuit mix, dry milk, and sugar (these could be pre-mixed) in a ziplocking bag.

3. Add egg and water. Mix well.

4. Open 1 corner of bag and squeeze batter over fruit cocktail.

batter

fruit

5. Cover skillet tightly. Cook slowly over fire 30-40 minutes.

6. Remove cover. Flip shortcake onto plate. Serve with cream, if desired.

By the Sea

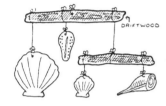

DRIFTWOOD

If you are visiting the seashore on your vacation, encourage your child to explore it with all of his senses. Most preschools and kindergartens offer a multi-sensory approach to learning and you should follow up on this approach whenever possible. The beach and the sea offer so many natural experiences that will appeal to your child.

There are hundreds of things to see at the seashore. Show your child how the water changes color at different times of the day. Observe the brightly colored sails on the boats on the horizon. Look at the beach towels and umbrellas. Let your child observe shells and pebbles and then wet them to see how they change color. Bring along a hand lens and let your child watch the little creatures—crabs, minnows, and periwinkles—in the tide pools at low tide.

Take some time to sit quietly together, close your eyes, and listen to the sounds of the seashore. Point out noises so your child hears the waves breaking, the water splashing, the cries of the gulls, motors on boats, children playing, people talking. Try listening together in the early morning and in the evening to see if you hear different sounds. Listen on a stormy day and talk with your child about the changes.

Take time to notice the smells of the beach with your child. The salt water combined with the scent of the fish and water plants is a very distinctive aroma. He may not like it very much, but be sure to let your child smell the beach at low tide.

Through his sense of touch, your child can explore the different textures at the seashore. Of course, sand—wet and dry—is a wonderful medium for play. As well as letting your child make castles and forts, have him get a stick and make shapes, numbers, and letters together in a smooth area of sand. Let your child experience—and talk about—other textures, too. Stones, pebbles, shells, seaweed—wet and dry—all of these have their own distinct textures. Encourage your child to describe how each one feels.

The beach is a wonderful place to start collections. Shells, pebbles, and other found treasures can be collected during the day and classified in the evening. Shells and pebbles can also be used for craft projects, such as decorating containers and mirrors. A lovely mobile can be made out of driftwood and shells.

TOGETHER

Sand can lead you to many interesting projects, like the one on the following page.

Of course, bring along sand and water toys whenever you go to the beach. Your child will be learning about weight, volume, and many other concepts while you relax and get a tan. Your most valuable input may be getting your child to talk about his explorations and discoveries—which will be numerous—at the seashore.

SAND CASTING

YOU'LL NEED:

- sand
- water
- shoe box *or* aluminum pie pan
- spoon
- large paper clips
- plaster of Paris
- bucket, pail, or empty coffee can
- shells
- pebbles
- buttons
- twigs

paper clip
plaster
COFFEE

WHAT TO DO:

1. Fill box or aluminum foil pan half way up with moist sand.

2. Make a design in sand, using finger or back of spoon.

3. Place pebbles, twigs, shells in or around design.

4. Mix plaster of Paris with water and pour it over entire surface.

Mix plaster in pail or empty coffee can.

5. When the plaster of Paris begins to harden, insert a large paper clip.

6. After the casting has hardened, lift it carefully out of the box or pie pan. Brush off excess sand.

use paper clip for a hanger.

On the Slopes

Are you heading for a ski vacation? Will it include your child? According to my ex-ski-patrolman husband who has raised three skier sons, *"If your child can skip, he can ski."* If your family consists of avid skiers, there is no reason why your child cannot start to learn to ski at three or four. The enthusiasm generated by other family members will rub off on a preschooler and can overshadow any doubts and fears he may have about this new experience. Even if everyone in the family is a beginner--like me--most children are ready to ski by five or six.

Before you head for the slopes, let your child become familiar with the clothing and equipment that are so important in this sport. Remember that comfort will be a major factor in your child's participation in skiing, so make sure that he is dressed warmly--but not so bundled up that he cannot move with ease. Heat escapes most from the head and hands, so hat and gloves must stay on while your child is out on the slopes. Let him help pick out these articles of clothing so that he is completely happy and comfortable with them. Goggles are also a must if it is snowing. Let your child wear his ski outfit in the backyard to play in the snow before you go away.

It is best to rent skis and boots for a young child until he is into the sport on a regular basis. Young children grow so quickly that you might be forced to buy new equipment each year. It is easy to rent equipment at the ski resorts or even local ski shops provide this service.

Once you arrive at the ski area, you have a choice: do you teach your child to ski yourself or enroll him in ski school. Your decision should be based on your level of competence--and just as important, patience. If you are not a practiced skier, put your child in ski school with a group of children his own age. The instructors will make the experience fun and your child will begin to learn the basics of skiing.

If you wish to teach your child yourself, find a small hill to begin on. If you are an expert skier, your very young child can ski down the hill between your skis or you can ski backwards holding his hands to guide him. Even a toddler can have fun doing this as long as his teacher is proficient and he feels steady and secure. Remember that young children have short attention spans so that lessons should last no longer than 20 minutes to half an hour--or whenever your child begins to feel tired or cold. Beware of wet fingers that can lead to frostbite. If you see whiteness on any of your child's extremeties, head for the nearest First Aid facility. Watch carefully for other signals that your child has had enough for one session--he has a lifetime of recreation ahead of him if he doesn't start off associating the sport with discomfort or boredom.

Chairlifts are novel, exciting, and dangerous for very young skiers. Discuss the rules thoroughly with the lift operator before you go on with your child. Always sit next to him on the chair. Be warned that getting off the chairlift is more difficult than getting on, so let a ski patrol member or other experienced skier help your child if you are not confident in your own ability.

Ski vacations offer your child more than skiing. Enjoy the snow together with the suggestions on page 38. Encourage your child to take in the experience with all of his senses--the smell of the pine trees, the glistening snow when the sun hits it, the swoosh of the skiers, the cold wetness as he fashions a snowball, the taste of hot chocolate when you go inside for a snack. Talk with him about his sensations--his vocabulary will expand along with his motor skills on the slopes.

HOLIDAYS 5

Fun or Frustration

Halloween

Pumpkin Power

Thanksgiving

'Tis the Season

Deck the Halls

Holiday Greetings

Gifts to Give and Make

Dec. 26—Jan. 2

Happy New Year

Valentine's Day, Hurrah!

Spring Celebrations

Patriotic Summer Holidays

Fun or Frustration

All of us experience many feelings at holiday times—happiness, excitement, anticipation, and sometimes sadness and even anxiety. Young children, who don't know what to expect, can feel fear when they should be feeling joy. It is especially important at these special times that you tune in to your child's emotions and try to provide as relaxed an atmosphere as possible in order to let everyone take part in the celebration at their own pace.

Sometimes you can avoid the whole subject with a toddler, but children three and over can usually sense that special occasions are coming. Helping your child sort out the time sequence can help him deal with his anticipation. Because a preschooler has little sense of time, he often needs you to explain how long it will be until the holiday. Always refer to a calendar and have your child circle the special day as a visual aid. You may be able to count out the days, but some children need to hear something like, *"You'll go to bed, get up, go to school, go home, go to sleep, get up, go to Scott's house to play, come home, go to bed, and then it will be Easter."* (three days from now) This may sound very repetitious, but it can really help your child understand the passage of time.

During holiday times, try to keep your child's routines as close to normal as possible. If everyday events—naptime, bedtime story, midmorning snack—occur as usual, your child will feel more secure even in the midst of special events, parties, and new people.

Most of us—including children—have our "best times" of the day. My daughter and I are both "morning people." Try to plan your child's involvement in holiday events around those times of day when he is most relaxed and receptive to new experiences. Don't introduce your child to a crowd of unfamiliar relatives or begin an exciting activity just before naptime, bedtime, or a regular mealtime.

Holiday mealtimes usually mean special foods—often rich, sweet, or spicy ones. Try to keep your child's menu as regular as his schedule. You can serve nutritious "everyday" foods party-style and your child will feel he is having a special meal. Also remember that most young children do not enjoy or belong at adult dinner parties. Let your child pass the hors d'oeuvres, talk with the guests, and perhaps choose a special relative to read his bedtime story BEFORE you sit down at the table. Your child will feel ripped off if he is whisked off to bed just as everyone else whisks off to dinner. A little preplanning can prevent a teary goodnight and a less-than-cheerful first course for your guests.

In this chapter, I will spotlight some of the major holidays with ideas for projects—many of which are easily adapted to other celebrations—to make the waiting fun and the special day, itself, a true learning adventures.

Make CELEBRATION BREAD on pages 100 and 101 once and your child will want to make it for every holiday. It's excellent practice in motor coordination, eye-hand coordination—and creativity. It's fun and practically foolproof, if you follow the directions. Just remember to use fresh yeast packets and dissolve in water 110 to 115 degrees F. Use a candy thermometer to test the warm water. As you set the yeast and water aside for the indicated three minutes, add 1/2 teaspoon of sugar. If the yeast is growing properly, it will start to bubble and foam. If it doesn't, something is wrong. Discard the yeast and start again.

You probably celebrate many holidays throughout the year, each one with its own special traditions, foods, music, games, and decorations. An excellent book that will give you ideas for 29 holidays is Festivals for You to Celebrate by Susan Purdy. The 85 craft projects can be used anytime you feel the need for a little celebration.

Remember that every day in the life of a young child has holiday potential. The first lost tooth, the first snow, the first tying of shoelaces—all of these are reasons for celebration. Don't let the calendar limit your fun.

CELEBRATION BREAD

YOU'LL NEED:

 2 packages yeast

 3/4 cup warm water

 2 Tblsp sugar or honey

 4½-5½ cups flour (white or mixed with a little whole wheat)

 1¼ cups buttermilk

 4 Tblsp. margarine

 2 tsp. baking powder

 2 tsp. salt

 bowls   mixing spoon

 waxed paper

 cookie sheet

OR

2 loaf pans

BASIC RECIPE

WHAT TO DO:

1. Combine yeast and warm water set aside for 3 minutes

2. In a bowl, combine 4½ cups flour, sugar, salt, baking powder, and margarine. Mix well.

3. Add yeast mixture to bowl.

4. Slowly add buttermilk and stir well. Dough should be soft but not sticky.

5. Knead 8 minutes.

6. Grease a cookie sheet or 2 loaf pans. Place dough in pans or shape on a cookie sheet.

7. Grease a large piece of waxed paper and cover dough. Let rise in a warm place for 45 minutes.

8. Remove waxed paper and place dough in preheated 400°F oven for 20-40 minutes. (20 minutes for small shaped loaves; 35-40 minutes for pan loaves.)

Great with a THANKSGIVING DINNER!

VARIATIONS

CHRISTMAS

knead into basic recipe:

½ cup NUTS (PINE NUTS are great)

½ cup RED and GREEN GLACEED CHERRIES

¼ cup SOFT RAISINS

CHANNUKAH

Shape bread dough into 3 balls. Roll each out long. Braid. Before baking, glaze with beaten EGG WHITE and 1 tsp WATER. Sprinkle with POPPY SEED.

VALENTINE'S DAY

Shape dough into 2 hearts on baking sheets. Bake and then glaze with POWDERED MILK FROSTING:

1. Cream 2 Tblsp. BUTTER and ⅓ CUP HONEY. Add 1 Tblsp. MILK and 1 tsp. VANILLA.

2. Blend in 3/4 cup POWDERED MILK (POWDER).

3. Add more MILK (liquid or dry) for right consistency.

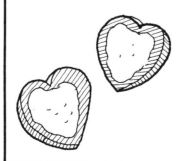

ST. PATRICK'S DAY

Take ⅓ of dough and knead in GREEN FOOD COLORING. Divide rest of dough into 3 large balls and 1 small ball. Press some green dough on each ball. Twist or press doughs together. Do not mix heavily. Shape balls into a SHAMROCK on a greased baking sheet. Bake.

EASTER

Shape dough into 3 balls. Roll each out long. Braid and shape braid into a circle. Dye RAW EGGS in Easter dyes. Place 4 or 5 eggs IN raised braid. Bake in oven for 35-45 minutes. Cool. Glaze with CONFECTIONER'S SUGAR and MILK combined. Sprinkle with pastel NONPAREILS.

Halloween

Halloween is a night for trick-or-treat, ghosts and goblins, and lots of fun. However, if you are not very careful, the fun can turn to fear and the pretend horrors can become all too real. This may be your child's first year to celebrate this spooky holiday. You can assure him a safe and enjoyable time, if you take certain precautions beforehand and during the evening.

Costumes can set the stage for fun or tragedy. Here are some DOs and DON'Ts.

▶ DON'T let your child wear a loose or oversized costume that he can trip over.

▶ DO have him wear everyday shoes, rather than high heel or costume shoes that may cause blisters.

▶ DON'T let him wear a full face mask which makes it hard for him to see traffic if he is going outside. Instead, use face paint or a lower face mask.

▶ DO use hair spray for weird hairdos, rather than wigs which are often made of flammable materials.

▶ DON'T let your child carry sharp or pointed toy weapons. He should have cardboard ones, if any.

▶ DO make or choose a light-colored costume, if your child is going from house to house. Then, it will be easier for drivers to see the child at night. If your child carries a flashlight and/or wears reflective strips, patches, or paint, he will be even more highly visible to cars.

▶ DON'T give your child a large, bulky trick-or-treat bag over which he can trip and fall. It also can block his vision or his body from an oncoming car.

If you buy a costume for your child, make sure it is made of flame-resistant material. However, part of the fun of Halloween for you and your child may be making the costume yourselves. A very young child will have more fun being creative than showing off a fancy store-bought creation. In addition, working on his own costume and mask can take some of the scariness out of wearing it later on and seeing others dressed up. Here are some ideas.

▶ He can be a BUNCH OF GRAPES. Buy some purple balloons. Tie each balloon to a piece of string and then, wind the string around your child's body. Cut out a green paper leaf and vine for him to wear on his head.

▶ He can be a SKELETON. Stick white adhesive tape to a dark shirt and slacks. Cover his head with black felt and use black and white face paint.

▶ Use cardboard boxes to make your child into a ROBOT, a TV SET, a BOX OF CEREAL, or PLAYING CARDS.

Have a dress rehearsal to make sure your child can move easily and see well. Also, talk over plans and rules in advance. Young children should go out in small groups of no more than three or four, always accompanied by an adult or older child. Dusk is the hardest time of day for motorists to see, so make sure your child understands and obeys the safety rules for walking

TOGETHER

Use paper bags to make easy, creative costumes. You might want to take a trip to the zoo before you decide on which animal to make. Add a foil-covered star and a red bandanna to the cowboy or cowgirl.

TOGETHER

PAPER BAG COSTUMES

YOU'LL NEED:

 scissors

glue

 yarn

permanent felt tip markers

brown paper lunch bags

brown paper grocery bags

WHAT TO DO:

1. ANIMALS

Cut 2 holes in a brown paper grocery bag for eyes. Cut up the sides so bag can be slipped over head and shoulders, leaving arms free. Decorate with yarn and markers.

2. COWBOY

Cut a brown paper grocery bag to make a **vest** and brown paper lunch bags for **leggings**. Add fringe from other brown bags.

3. COWGIRL

Cut a brown paper grocery bag to make a **vest**. Cut another brown paper grocery bag for a **skirt**. Add fringe from other brown bags.

yarn

child-eye level holes

VEST

LEGGINGS (lunch bags cut open and glued end to end.)

VEST

cut a hole

SKIRT

the street. Remember that he will be excited and thus probably less careful than he normally is. Make sure that he knows to:

▪ Cross at the crosswalk
▪ Wait for the proper signal
▪ Look both ways before crossing
▪ Be alert for turning cars at an intersection
▪ Never go into the street between parked cars
▪ Stay on the sidewalk, whenever possible, and if there is no sidewalk, walk to the left where he faces the traffic

Unfortunately, dangerous treats have become a real problem in the past few years. Have your child bring home ALL the treats he collects for you to inspect. Make up a special goody bag for him to take and munch from as he goes from house to house, so he won't be tempted by anything he collects. Wash and cut up all fruit collected. Throw out all unpacked or loosely wrapped items, like popcorn or small candies.

Halloween Party

With all the potential dangers on Halloween, you might consider getting together with other families in your neighborhood, nursery school, daycare center, or playgroup, and organizing a Halloween party at one person's home. Have each parent bring enough treats for each child; the children can go trick-or-treating from room to room.

Plan some age-appropriate, fun activities for your spooky celebration.

▶ Tape record some "scary" sounds to be played as background "sound effects." Sounds like rattling chains, a meowing cat, loud footsteps, creaking doors, moans, and groans, will bring excitement and laughter without being frightening. You may want to have the children try to identify the sounds as a group and perhaps add their own scary sounds to the tape.

▶ Tape some large sheets of drawing paper, newsprint, or cut-up grocery bags child-height on a wall, provide children with crayons or markers, and let each child make a scary picture. When they are through, they will have created a Halloween mural. If you give the children glow-in-the-dark markers, the effect will be terrific when you turn off the lights.

▶ Now that you—and the children—have created the proper atmosphere, it's time to play a game. Ask everyone to form a circle and play "The Goblin in the Dark" with words sung to the tune of "The Farmer in the Dell." One child, who stands in the center of the circle, is the "goblin." Everyone circles the goblin and sings, *"The goblin in the dark, the goblin in the dark, Heigh-ho, it's Halloween, the goblin in the dark."* As the children march around, the goblin takes a ghost; the ghost takes a witch; the witch a cat, and so on, until the center is filled with creepy characters.

▶ Have a snack and after the children have eaten, sing a song to the tune of "Ten Little Indians." *"One little, two little, three little pumpkins; four little, five little, six little pumpkins; seven little, eight little, nine little pumpkins; ten*

TOGETHER

Create homemade Trick or Treat Bags either before or at the Halloween Party.

TRICK OR TREAT BAG

YOU'LL NEED:

 scissors

 stapler

 grocery bag

 crayons or felt tip markers

 reflective tape

 12" x 2" strip of cardboard

WHAT TO DO:

 1. Cut bag shape from grocery bag.

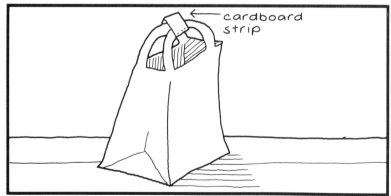

 2. Staple both handles together. Reinforce with a strip of cardboard folded and stapled to center of the 2 handles.

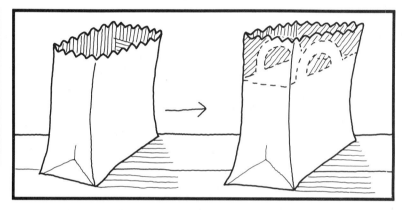

cardboard strip

 3. Draw Jack O' Lanterns, cats, and other designs on bag. If possible, stick on reflective tape.

With your child, make these individual Jack-o'-lantern Fruit Cups for everyone to enjoy at the party.

pumpkins on the fence." You can sing about *"witches flying in the sky," "cats in a tree," and "ghosts in the dark."*

► Take each child's picture with an instant-developing camera before they leave. This will be a memento of a good, safe Halloween.

At the end of the day (and perhaps to prepare your child the week before) read together some books on Halloween like The Mystery of the Flying Pumpkin by Steven Kellog.

JACK--LANTERN FRUIT CUP

YOU'LL NEED:

 orange

 fruits

 toothpick

felt tip marker

spoon

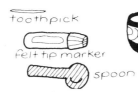 bowl

 plastic knife (for children to use)

metal knife (ADULT USE ONLY)

WHAT TO DO:

1. Adult cuts off top of orange

2. Scoop out insides and put into bowl

3. Using a plastic knife, cut fruits.

4. Fill scooped out orange with fruits

scooped out orange

bowl of cut fruit

5. Replace top of orange. Stick together with a toothpick

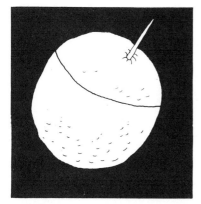

6. Draw on a face with a marker

Pumpkin Power

While you're carving your jack-o'-lantern, let me say a word about pumpkins. They're an important part of all the holidays in fall, and they can be used for many learning experiences.

The pumpkin seeds you scoop out can provide hours of learning fun. Your child can count them and once they are dried, he can paste them on cardboard to make number cards. These cards can be used for counting, learning sets, and for playing matching games. He can also use the seeds for collages and for just creating designs.

Dried pumpkin seeds can be strung together with strong thread and a blunt needle to make jewelry. Roasted pumpkin seeds make delicious snacks.

Your child can save a few pumpkin seeds to plant in the garden in late spring. Read a book on gardening for instructions. Don't expect instant results—they have a long growing season, but if you are lucky, you will have a homegrown jack-o'-lantern the following October. (The first year we tried this, we got no results at all. The next year, however, we had a huge vine growing out of the compost pile.)

Your child can practice his woodworking skills by hammering nails into a pumpkin. When he is first learning to use a hammer, the tough rind almost assures a successful experience.

TOGETHER

Pumpkin Butter is a good, spicy treat that is easy to make and spread on thick slices of homemade bread.

Pieces of pumpkin cut into various shapes and sizes can be used for printing. You may also cut designs into the smooth outer surface of pumpkin chunks. Make a paint pad by folding a wet cloth or paper towel in a shallow dish. Sprinkle it with powdered paint or brush on tempera paint. Press cut pumpkin into paint pad and then down on paper to make a print. Your child can experiment with designs and repeating patterns. Pumpkin prints can be used for holiday wrapping paper, stationery, tags, or cards.

For more ideas and information on pumpkins, read The All-Around Pumpkin Book by Maggie Cuyler and From Seed to Jack-o'-lantern by Hannah Johnson.

PUMPKIN BUTTER

YOU'LL NEED:

 pumpkin

1 cup molasses

CINNAMON 1 tsp. cinnamon

NUTMEG 1/4 tsp. nutmeg

sharp knife - ADULT USE ONLY

GINGER 1/4 tsp. ginger

CLOVES 1/4 tsp. cloves

water

spoon

WHAT TO DO:

1. Adult cuts pumpkin in half.

2. Take seeds out of pumpkin.

3. Add a little water to pumpkin half.

4. Bake pumpkin in 350° F oven for 1 hour or until soft.

5. Scoop out cooked pumpkin and cook with the other ingredients, stirring all the time, until thick and buttery.

6. Spread on bread or crackers.

Thanksgiving

If you're preparing a family feast for Thanksgiving, let your child help out. As you plan, shop, cook, and serve together, your child can do a lot of learning.

Let your child help you plan the menu. Discuss what is served every year as part of the tradition (turkey and stuffing, pumpkin pie) and let him choose some other dishes. Let him make his choices within your framework of the meal. For example, tell him you're going to serve potatoes. *"Should it be mashed potatoes or sweet potatoes? Would you prefer carrots or turnips?"*

At the Market

Once you have decided on a menu, take your child along when you go shopping. Give him the responsibility of finding a few items on your list. In the produce department, let your child tell you the colors and shapes of the fruits and vegetables. Encourage him to choose two foods, guess which one is heavier, and then weigh them on the produce scale to see if he was correct. (This is a math lesson!)

If there is a bakery department in the supermarket, challenge your child to guess what's in the oven before you reach the counter. A freshly baked cookie makes a good reward for the right answer.

Especially at holiday times, checkout lines can be very long—much longer than your child's patience. Here are some games to play as you wait in line.

▶ Play "I spy." The market is full of items that lend themselves to sensory descriptions. *"I spy something that is yellow and round and juicy and tastes sour."* (a grapefruit) Take turns giving clues and guessing.
▶ Bring along a small pad and marker and let your child make tallie of items, people in line, magazines in the rack at the counter—even types of cereal on the shelves as you pass through the aisle together.
▶ NEVER let your child out of your sight in a public place, such as a supermarket. Too many children disappear because their parents let them wander off "just for a moment." It may take a bit more time, but always stay with your child when he wishes to look at something in a store. Don't send him to a different part of the store to fetch something you forgot. Children have been known to disappear when they were only an aisle away from their parents.
▶ When you arrive at the checkout counter, have your child hand you the items from the cart as you name them. Identify the money, especially the coins you use to pay for your purchases. If you have a coupon, let your child match it to the correct item and hand it to the cashier.

INDIAN PUDDING

YOU'LL NEED:

 1/4 cup storebought cornmeal

2 stones for grinding

OO 2 eggs

 1 package frozen corn nibblets

3/4 cup molasses

1 tsp. salt (or less)

 1 tsp. cinnamon

1/2 tsp ginger

1 cup cold milk

 2 Tblsp. butter

4 cups hot milk

baking pan (12" x 18" x 2")

pan in pan-like double boiler

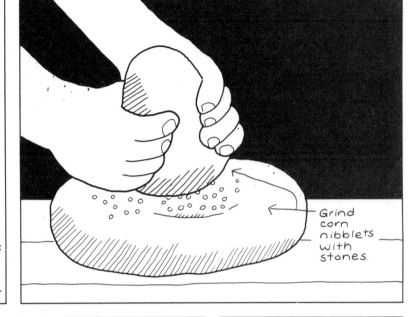

Grind corn nibblets with stones.

WHAT TO DO:

1.
Make your own GROUND CORNMEAL. Use 2 stones to grind it. 1 stone should be flat with a hollow in the middle, the other should be rounded and heavy.

2.
Then, place a package of frozen corn nibblets in the oven on a cookie sheet. Dry out in a low (150°-200°F) oven. When hard and dry, grind to meal.

3.
Slowly, stir 1/4 cup homemade cornmeal and 1/4 cup storebought cornmeal into hot milk. Milk should be in a pan over another pan of boiling water (like a double boiler).

4.
Cook hot milk and cornmeal for 20 minutes.

5.
Add the rest of the ingredients (except the cold milk) to the cornmeal mixture.

6.
Pour mixture into a 12" x 18" x 2" pan. Pour 1 cup cold milk over it. DO NOT MIX. Bake at 325°F for 50 minutes. Serve warm.

Preparing the Meal

Of course, the biggest part of this project is preparing the dinner. Make whatever you can ahead of time. Try to space out the preparation time, so that your young helper doesn't lose interest. There are so many things he can do: tear bread for stuffing, scrub potatoes, peel onions–unless his eyes start to water or sting–knead dough for rolls, break eggs and mix them with a hand beater, you'll think of many more small, but necessary, jobs.

As you cook, read the recipes aloud to show your child one more practical use of reading and following directions. As always, talk about the textures, smells, tastes, and the colors of the ingredients. Compare raw and cooked potatoes and pie dough before and after baking. Talk about how foods change when they have been in the oven or the freezer. (It's science!)

Let your child help you measure ingredients by putting a rubber band around the measuring cup to mark the amount you need. Count and describe the quantities you use and the sizes of the dishes, bowls, and cups. Talk about cooking time. You can use a kitchen timer to time many cooking activities. *"Beat the batter until the buzzer goes off."* Preparing a family feast gives you so many opportunities to introduce math concepts.

Turkey Day

On Thanksgiving Day, let your child help you set the table and serve some of the food. Let everyone know that he helped with the cooking. He will be proud to have been part of the process in the real spirit of that first Thanksgiving, where work and cooperation created a feast for everyone.

In many families, Thanksgiving means a large family gathering. For the adults in the family, this means a time to renew old acquantances and reminisce, but, to a young child, it means meeting many new people and being involved in a new, often intimidating experience. Relatives and friends you have known and loved all your life are often strangers to your child. Being sensitive to and understanding of your child's feelings and moods at a family gathering can save embarrassment on your part and unhappiness on the part of your child. Take your child aside or into another room periodically during the party to "check things out" and answer any questions he might have about people or what is happening.

One way to ease the strain of meeting so many new people is to "introduce them in advance." Talk about relationships, *"Uncle Roger is Grandma's brother, just like Chris is your brother,"* and tell stories about when you were the same age as your child, *"I used to stay overnight with Uncle Roger and Aunt Peggy; I played checkers with them."* Illustrate your stories with old pictures and your child will be enchanted. You can introduce visitors from far away over the phone or through postcards.

Be sure to tell your child exactly who will be at the party. He can help you make placecards or even small gifts to give each guest.

Don't expect your child to sit through a two-hour, grown-up dinner party listening politely to adult conversation. Because the nerves and circulation systems in their bodies have not completely developed, it is not possible for most young children to be still for more than ten and, at the most, twenty minutes at a time. When they are not the center of attention, you must cut this time down. So, as long as your child is being quiet and well-behaved, cross your fingers and do nothing. But, have distractions on hand for when he becomes bored (inevitably and with reason).

Know the group of people at the table. If they are informal, they probably won't mind your child quietly playing with small toys, puzzles, and games on the table (*"You must keep the puzzle on your placemat between the fork and knife"*). In many cases, it is better for him to be excused between courses to play on the floor or in another room.

At bedtime, try these books about Thanksgiving: <u>Over the River and Through the Woods</u>, which features the words with which your child is probably familiar with, along with old-fashioned illustrations; <u>Chester Chipmunk's Thanksgiving</u> by Barbara Williams; and <u>The Thanksgiving Book</u> by Frank Jupo.

'Tis the Season

December is a time for celebration. Whether your family celebrates Christmas, Hanukkah—the Jewish festival of lights, or Kwanza—an Afro-American holiday, this is a month for giving, receiving, family togetherness, and lots of fun.

It can also be a time of overexcitement, confusion, and high anxiety for your child. Picture this scene: all the store windows are decorated; inside the shelves burst with toys and gifts; at dusk, the streets light up. What holiday is rapidly approaching? THANKSGIVING. Each year, it seems children have longer to wait between the time Santa appears in the stores and the time he actually comes down the chimney. It's no wonder the little sense of time they have is confused and the waiting seems endless.

There are ways to help your child pass the time—and understand that time is passing. You can create a darling takeoff on the traditional advent calendar by making a large picture of a lamb or Santa face. (If you have no faith in your drawing skills, cut a picture out of a magazine.) Count out a cotton ball or piece of popcorn for every day until the holiday and put them in a see-through container. Have your child glue one on the picture each day.

When the container is empty, it's holiday time—and your child has been able to really "see" the time pass!

Try to plan small "special events" before the big one. Go caroling; bake holiday cookies; visit stores or the mall to look at decorations—no shopping allowed. Add these special events to your calendar so that the wait for the "big day or days" doesn't seem so long.

Your child will love helping you prepare for the holidays. Most children will channel some of the energy from their anticipation into making decorations, helping prepare make-ahead foods, and creating cards, invitations, and thank-you notes. One little boy deals with his anticipation of Christmas by decorating all of the window panes in his house. Every day before Dec. 25, he takes his crayons, paper, scissors, and tape and makes decorations. Some days he does one window pane, other times a whole window, and other times a whole room. He doesn't really care if he finishes the whole house by Christmas; this is his own special way of dealing with a holiday over which he usually has little control.

So, let your child do something each day before a holiday, beginning when you sense his need for an energy outlet. Let him work through his excitement, anticipation—and sometimes fear—and have creative learning experiences at the same time. Use the activities which follow or refer to some of these excellent books.

- Christmas Fun by Judith Hoffman Corwin
- Things to Make and Do for Christmas by Ellen Weiss
- Jewish Holiday Gifts by Joyce Becker

TOGETHER

Create an imaginative Felt Board Calendar to count the days until that most special time.

FELT BOARD CALENDAR

YOU'LL NEED:

- 1 piece of felt 36"x 24" (white or red)
- 1 piece of felt, dark green, 24"x 24"
- 1 piece of Cardboard, 36"x 24" OR
- scraps of bright colored felt
- 1 piece of felt, black, 10"x 12" OR
- needle and thread
- scissors
- yarn
- glue
- dowel
- fabric marker

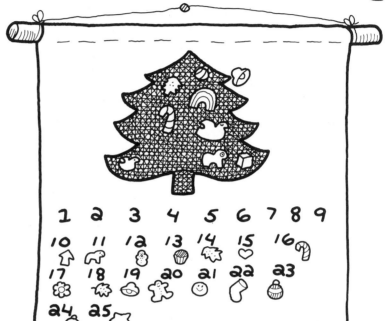

WHAT TO DO:

1. Glue the red or white felt to a 36"x 24" piece of cardboard OR sew a small pocket at 24" side and slip in a dowel.

2. Poke 2 holes in felt-covered cardboard and tie with yarn to hang OR tie yarn around dowel and hang.

3. Cut a Christmas tree shape (appx. 22"x 22") from green felt. Glue tree onto red or white background, near the top.

4. Using black felt, cut out numbers, 1-25. Glue numbers in calendar form under tree OR use a fabric marker and write in numbers.

5. Cut out 25 simple ornament shapes.

6. Place 1 ornament next to each number. Each day, place 1 on the tree. Save the star for last.

Deck the Halls

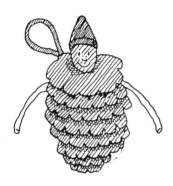

Part of the joy of the holidays comes from the decorations in our homes, stores, churches, synagogues, streets, and schools in December. Homemade decorations seem to embody the spirit of the season and evoke wonderful holiday memories each year they are displayed. Here are some decorations that are easy and fun to make with your child. Let your child do as much of each project as possible by himself.

Make ELVES FROM PINECONES by gluing an acorn to the bottom of a pine cone. This is now the head of the elf. Make a hat from a semicircle of red felt or paper, glued into a cone shape. Make a face with markers and add arms with a twisted pipe cleaner. To hang, glue on a loop of red yarn.

Read the delightful The Shoemaker and the Christmas Elves by Jane Belk Moncure.

▶ CLOTHESPIN ANGELS are festive additions to a tree, table, or hanging from a bannister. To make one, poke a hole in the center of a lace doily and put a wooden clothespin through it so that the doily becomes a lacy gown. The rounded part of the clothespin becomes the head. Glue the doily around the neck area.

Glue puffs of polyester stuffing or cotton to the back of the head to be hair. Draw a face on the clothespin with markers. Sprinkle glitter on the hair or make a halo from a twisted gold pipecleaner.

Take a second doily and pinch together in the center to make wings. Glue to the back of the angel. To hang, tie on a loop of heavy white thread.

▶ Read Cobweb Christmas by Shirley Climo to your child and create some SPIDER WEB STARS together. First, dilute some white glue with a few drops of water and place in a wide, flat container like an aluminum pie tin. Cut pieces of white yarn or string into lengths of eight to ten inches. Let your child dip pieces of yarn or string into the glue, covering thoroughly. Place string pieces on waxed paper, creating a multi-pointed star effect. Cut one 18-inch piece of string, and have your child dip it into the glue and then spiral it around the star shapes. Let it dry overnight and then peel it off the waxed paper. When you add a piece of string as a hanger, these make beautiful tree ornaments.

▶ A SNOWMAN SNACK SERVER is a festive way to serve holiday goodies. To make one, you'll need three small, white, flat paper plates. On one plate, have your child make a snowman face. On the second plate, have them make branchlike arms and coal-black buttons. Set the third blank plate on a flat surface and staple the second plate with the arms and buttons to its rim so it stands up. Staple the plate with the face to the "body" plate so the snowman is standing tall. Have your child cut a top hat from black construction paper and staple it on the head. Tie on a red crepe paper streamer for a scarf. Use this plate for holiday snacks; the weight of the food keeps the snowman standing up.

TOGETHER

Make up ornament kits in shoeboxes to take out when your child needs a pre-holiday project.

ORNAMENTS

GLITTER ORNAMENTS

1. Glue glitter onto pinecones, cardboard shapes, and styrofoam balls.

2. HINT: Put glue in a styrofoam meat tray. Put glitter into another. Roll object in glue and then in glitter.

3. Add ribbon or yarn to hang ornaments.

BREAD DOUGH ORNAMENTS

1. mix together: 4 cups flour, 1 cup salt, 1½ cups warm water.

2. knead 10 minutes. keep covered in plastic wrap.

3. Form shapes using water to join pieces of dough.

4. Place on cookie sheets. Bake at 300°F for 1-1½ hours.

5. Paint on features with acrylic paint. coat with polyurethane or spray acrylic.

TIN ORNAMENTS

1. Draw designs on aluminum pie plates, roasting pans or t.v. dinner trays.

2. Using scissors, cut out designs

3. Hammer nail holes all around design.

4. Put a string through 1 hole to hang the ornament.

Holiday Greetings

You and your child can create unique holiday greetings for any holiday, but December is a particularly appropriate time to send good wishes to friends and relatives. Here are some fun ways to "send your very best."

▶ For friends with a sweet tooth, your child can make GUMDROP CARDS. Together, make a frosting glue of one cup confectioners' sugar and the white of one egg. Use this frosting to glue gumdrops to folded construction paper in the form of a design, letter, or object. The gumdrops can be peeled off and eaten by the recipient.

▶ SPONGE PRINTS make terrific cards. First, have your child cut out some appropriate holiday objects. Place the cutouts on a folded piece of construction paper. Sponge tempera paint all over the paper. Let dry. When you remove the cutouts, you will have a card with holiday silhouettes. This technique makes handsome wrapping paper, too.

▶ You can use your child's HANDPRINT to make many personalized cards. One handprint and with a few marker details make a Thanksgiving turkey. Use the side of his hand and five fingerprints to make a footprint.

▶ Use the stamp pad to make WRAPPING PAPER, also. Dip cookie cutters, vegetable cutouts, or stamps (store-bought or made from inner tube rubber, if you're ambitious) into paint and then press them onto heavy butcher paper or grocery bags slit open. Place decorated paper on several layers of newspaper to dry.

Here are three ideas for holiday THANK-YOU NOTES.

▶ Take a photo of your child playing with his gift or wearing a gift of clothing. You might also want to include a sign in the picture, saying "Thanks!"

▶ With your child, make giant cookies from your favorite recipe. When cooled, write with frosting: *Thank you, from _____ (your child's name)."* Wrap each cookie in plastic and tie with yarn.

▶ Your child will love making this pop-out kiss card for a favorite friend who lives far away. Have him accordion-fold a piece of 1/2 inch-wide paper that is about five inches long. Let your child cut out a big pair of paper lips and color them bright red. He can tape the folded paper "spring" to the right side of a folded piece of construction paper and glue the lips onto the top fold. Let your child decorate the cover of the card. You can write inside, *"A Great Big Kiss for your Great Gift!"*

TOGETHER

Make these Holiday Cards together. Use them as greetings or thank-you notes. The dots can be bubbles, balloons, or snowflakes by adding a few lines.

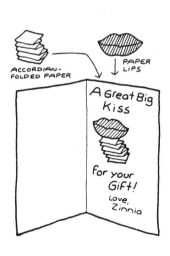

ACCORDIAN-FOLDED PAPER

PAPER LIPS

A Great Big Kiss

for your Gift!

Love, Zinnia

HOLIDAY CARDS

YOU'LL NEED:

new pencil with eraser • white poster paint • construction paper- white, red, green, blue • tissue paper • gift wrap • scissors • glue • yarn • bird seed

WHAT TO DO: WHITE DOT CARDS

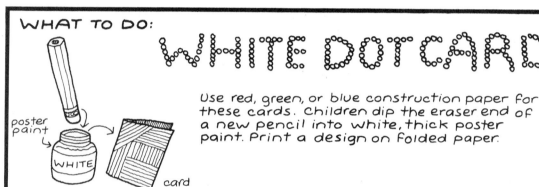

poster paint → WHITE → card

Use red, green, or blue construction paper for these cards. Children dip the eraser end of a new pencil into white, thick poster paint. Print a design on folded paper.

BIRD CARDS

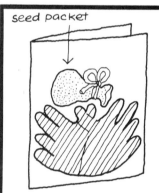

seed packet

Trace both hands of a child, so they overlap like this:

Make the "birds" red. Cut them out and glue onto white paper. Take a circle of tissue paper and fill with bird seed. Tie with yarn like a sack. Glue seed bag in place as if a bird were carrying it.

PATCHWORK PRETTIES

Cut up many different print gift wrap papers into triangles, squares, and rectangles. Each shape should be no more than 1½"- 2" wide.

Have children glue them down onto cover of folded paper to form a patchwork quilt-like design.

Gifts to Give

Several times a year, you give gifts to people. Whether you buy or make them, choosing presents is a challenge. It can be a real problem for your child, who has had little experience doing it. It's up to you to help him understand that it's not how large the gift is or how much is spent, but rather the feelings behind it. Something he makes or something he does for someone is appreciated much more than an expensive store-bought item.

Help your child think about the person for whom the gift is intended—what he likes, what might be appropriate because of the season or the occasion. Make sure he understands that a homemade gift doesn't have to be perfect; it's the thought that counts!

TOGETHER

Sometimes, the perfect gift is not an item, but a service. Encourage your child to give of himself by making this gift certificate.

During your discussion about gifts, go to the library and find Oatmeal Is Not for Mustaches by Thomas Rockwell. Together with your child, enjoy the hilarious ideas for special gifts—unusual uses for everyday items. The Christmas Box by Eve Merriam is another children's story that will spark your child's imagination.

Parenting educator Ellen Goldstein suggests that you sit down with your child during the gift-giving season, and make a chart like the one below. Write down your child's ideas and help him make a decision. This is also wonderful practice in thinking skills and concept formation.

PERSON GIFT IS FOR:	OCCASION:	AGE:	THINGS I KNOW THEY LIKE:	THINGS I COULD MAKE OR DO:
Mother	Birthday	Adult	Stationery, books, candles, candle-holders, plants, painting	stenciled gift wrap for small gifts. clay candle holder. plant a clay pot or make a terrarium.
Father	Father's Day	Adult	sports jogging, books, taking pictures.	bookmark. my own picture pasted on cardboard, framed with yarn.
Sister	Birthday	10 years old	dolls, music, dancing, skating, hamburgers.	GIFT CERTIFICATE of my services- take on her job of setting the table for 1 week. GIFT CERTIFICATE at her favorite restaurant for a free hamburger.

GIFT CERTIFICATE

THIS GIFT CERTIFICATE IS GOOD FOR:

One week of setting the table
_____

FROM: Your Sister, Kim   FOR: Rachel
_____   _____
Name of gift-giver   Name of gift receiver

AND MAY BE REDEEMED: Anytime after christmas
                                    _____
                                    Date/period of time

   SIGNED BY: Kim
                                                    _____
                                                    Name of gift-giver

MAKE COPY AND
CUT ALONG BROKEN LINE.

GIFT CERTIFICATE

THIS GIFT CERTIFICATE IS GOOD FOR :

_____

FROM: _____   FOR: _____

AND MAY BE REDEEMED: _____

          SIGNED BY:
                              _____

Gifts to Mak

As I said before, try to encourage your child to make his own holiday gifts, rather than buying them. Use the projects, mentioned throughout this book for ideas. If he knows someone who lives someplace warm, he might want to make them the FAN on page 73. The POTPOURRI on page 37 makes a lovely gift for his grandparents. He might want to make the KITE on page 43 for a cousin or a friend.

A lovely MINI-GARDEN can be made out of a simple soda bottle. It's a perfect gift for someone who loves gardening in the warmer months. Take a two-liter, plastic soda bottle that comes apart into two sections and remove the bottom by filling it with very hot water. Cut off the neck of the bottle with scissors. Place potting soil in the bottom portion of the container. Have your child choose some small plants, rocks, and figures to arrange in the soil. Water well. Replace the plastic top and decorate with a colorful bow. This mini-greenhouse needs watering only two or three times a month. Be sure to include a tag with instructions for its care.

Gifts of food are also a treat to make and give. Make gingerbread men or a gingerbread house to give as a gift. The GRAHAM CRACKER HOUSE on page 125 is an easy, but creative, alternative. Be sure to read The Gingerbread Man or Hansel and Gretel when you're done cooking.

TOGETHER

Your child will be amazed by this project, as big pictures shrink to tiny miniatures. Shrinkies make lovely gifts as jewelry or magnets or ornaments for a Christmas tree. Other holiday gift projects follow on the next four pages.

During the holidays, be sure to make quiet times to read stories and reflect on the many exciting events. For Hanukkah, read Potato Pancakes All Around by Marilyn Hirsch. It's a fun-filled tale that even includes a recipe, if you don't have a family favorite. Hirsch has written another delightful book for the holidays called I Love Hanukkah. A Picture Book of Jewish Holidays by David Adler gives simple facts about Hanukkah, as well as other celebrations.

To get in the Christmas spirit, read The Friendly Beasts by Tomie dePaola, which tells part of the nativity story from the point of view of the animals in the manger. The Church Mice at Christmas by Graham Oakley is the amusing story of how some mice decide that their holidays would be nicer if they had a big party. Their efforts to raise money will take your child's mind off any anxieties. Christmas illustrated by Jan Pienkowski and Spirit Child by Bierhorst are both simple and beautiful retellings of the nativity story that you can share with your child. It's important to share the lovely, peaceful parts of the holiday that are far removed from the tinsel, toys, and the *"Ho, ho, ho's"* of Santa, especially when your child is feeling overwhelmed by the material aspects of the season.

SHRINKIES

YOU'LL NEED:

 Styrofoam meat trays (get clean ones from the butcher)

 felt tip markers (permanent ones are best)

 scissors

 glue

 baking sheet

 spatula

small magnets, string, clasp

 aluminum foil

WHAT TO DO:

1. Draw a picture on a styrofoam meat tray with markers.

2. Cut it out. Poke a hole in it for an ornament or pendant.

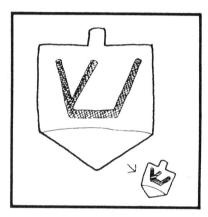

3. Place on a foil-covered baking sheet.

4. Adult places cut-out shape in 300°F oven for 3-5 minutes. Watch carefully. If, at the end of 5 minutes, piece has curled, adult can use a spatula to flatten.

5. Remove from oven and cool. It will be small and hard.

6. Add string for a pendant or an ornament, a magnet for a refrigerator note holder, a clasp for a decorative jewelry pin.

DREIDEL-SHAPED MENORAH

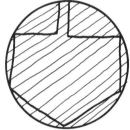 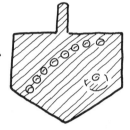

YOU'LL NEED:

 self-hardening clay

rolling pin

plastic knife

birthday candles

WHAT TO DO:

1. Roll out self-hardening clay like a pancake and pound it down to about ½" thickness.

2. Cut out dreidel shape with plastic knife.

3. Push in 8 little holes with a birthday candle.

4. With some extra clay, make a mound for the SHAMMUS, the ninth candle that sits above the others.

5. Push in a little hole in the mound for the SHAMMUS.

6. Stick a birthday candle in each hole.

HOLIDAY CRAFTS

SNOW JAR

1. Cut a 2" x 2" piece of aluminum foil into tiny squares.
2. Place flower into jar upside down.
3. Place foil squares into jar and fill jar to overflowing with water.
4. Close tightly and shake.

baby food jar →

plastic flower

HANDPRINT WREATH

1. Cover child's hand with green poster paint.
2. On a piece of 12" x 12" muslin, print hand around in a circle to resemble a wreath.
3. Child uses his thumb dipped in red poster paint and stamps holly berries around wreath.
4. Glue top to a dowel and string with yarn.

PAPER STOCKING

1. Cut 2 large stocking shapes from paper. Punch holes through both parts all around.
2. Wrap 1 end of a piece of yarn with tape and use yarn to lace up sides.
3. Fill with hand drawn toys

CRANBERRY-ORANGE RELISH

YOU'LL NEED:

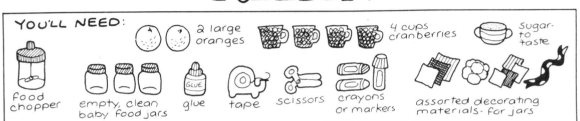

2 large oranges

4 cups cranberries

sugar-to-taste

food chopper

empty, clean baby food jars

glue

tape

scissors

crayons or markers

assorted decorating materials- for jars

WHAT TO DO:

construction paper rolled into tube and taped- for head

draw on a face

baby food jar filled with relish

cotton ball

ribbon

paper or fabric scrap mittens

cotton ball or fabric beard

SAMPLE CRANBERRY-ORANGE RELISH JAR

1. Divide oranges into 1/8's. Remove seeds.

2. Put orange sections and cranberries through the coarse blade of a food chopper. Add sugar- to taste.

3. Store in clean, empty baby food jars. Decorate the jar.

GIFTS OF FOOD

YUMMY TABLE TOP TREE

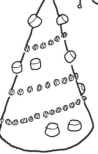

1. Use a cone-shaped ice cream cone turned upside down.

2. Combine 1/4 cup margarine, 2 tsp. milk, 2 cups confectionary sugar and green food coloring.

3. Frost cone and trim with raisins, nuts, and mini-marshmallows.

GRAHAM CRACKER HOUSE

1. Make a ROYAL FROSTING by beating 3 egg whites to a frothy foam and add 1 lb. confectionery sugar and a few drops of lemon juice.

2. Attach graham crackers to empty milk cartons with frosting.

3. Frost crackers and trim with nuts, candy, raisins, and chocolate chips.

PEANUT BUTTER SNOWBALLS

1. Combine 1 cup peanut butter with 1/2 cup dry milk powder, and a few Tblsp. honey to moisten.

2. Chill mixture 1/2 - 1 hour.

3. Roll into balls and roll balls in shredded coconut.

Gifts for Your Child

The stores are full of the "right toys for any child." But, what are the right toys for YOUR child? I don't know your child, so I wouldn't venture to say, but I can give you some general guidelines that have helped me choose appropriate toys for my child and others.

▶ First, spend some time observing your child before you set out to buy gifts. Avoid the temptation to run for your pad and pencil each time he's watching TV ads and cries, *"I want that."* Unfortunately, our children are programmed to ask for things simply because they see them on TV. Sometimes, my daughter won't even know what it is she is asking for, but the picture of happy (often older) kids joyfully opening a box to find that particular toy is very seductive. Take the time to probe a bit, *"What is that? Why do you want it?"* Toys often look bigger and brighter on TV than they do in actuality. Help your child become a conscientious consumer by showing him the toy in the store. *"Does this toy look like the one on TV?"*

▶ Check toys out for durability and safety. Make sure that replacement parts are obtainable and that the plastic in toys is heavy and doesn't crack easily. Look out for sharp edges (I know a nine-month-old who got a paper cut every time she played with a seemingly harmless plastic book.), long cords that could strangle a curious toddler, toys with moving parts that could pinch or catch in hair or on clothing, parts that could break or fall off and be swallowed, and toys without a nontoxic label.

▶ A word about small toys or toys with lots of small parts. Think about the whole family, not just the child for whom you are purchasing the gift, when you buy a toy or game. It may not be wise to give a puzzle with 60 small pieces to a five-year-old who has a nine-month-old brother.

▶ Find out which toys your child enjoys the most and find out if additions are available. If your child is a big builder, maybe there are new pieces on sale for his building set. If he has a favorite doll, perhaps there are accessories available. Find toys and games with many uses. Toy manufacturers are particulary sensitive to the need for multi-purpose playthings, so try to read the instructions or box copy for ideas. Many times, your child will invent his own ways to use a toy, his own rules for a game. Don't restrict him with *"But this is the way you play..."* Let him explore the possibilities and develop his creative thinking skills at the same time.

If your child is anything like mine, he has a room full of toys and still prefers to play with pots and pans in the kitchen or the hole puncher in my desk. Children learn through imitation and their most intriguing learning tools are the ones they see us, the important adults in their lives, using. Try hunting for holiday gifts in places other than the local toy store.

▶ Buy your child his own hole puncher in your local stationery store. Add an inexpensive label maker, interesting pencils, markers (fat and thin), small, multi-colored notepads, reinforcements, paper clips, and pack them all in an accordion file. Your child has all the ingredients for a mini-office. Keep him supplied with junk mail to open, mark up, and file, and he will be set for hours of dramatic play.

Put together an artist's kit from an art store. Assemble multi-shaped plastic stencils; construction paper; stick-on stars, letters, and circles; and, perhaps, a special rubber stamp with your child's name and a stamp pad. Attach everything to a clipboard and let your little artist go to work.

A large-sized nut and bolt from the hardware store make a fine puzzle for a toddler. Older children will enjoy a carpentry box with a good quality hammer, nails, soft wood, and glue. Add bottle caps, corks, markers, yarn, and glitter and your child will have lots to fuel his creative thinking. Try <u>Easy Woodstuff for Kids</u> by David Thompson for ideas. Other hardware-store gifts include: a retractable tape measure, a padlock and key, and a flashlight with batteries. A metal lockbox with key makes a perfect treasure chest.

ART SUPPLIES

Go into the fabric store to create a sewing box for your child. Include cut squares of burlap and felt, blunt-end yarn needles, buttons, lace, ribbons, sequins, glue, yarn, and fabric scraps. Since you will need to supervise your child's use of needles, this gift leads to many special times.

Try the local nursery for the perfect gardener's kit. A few packages of seeds, a small trowel, some clay pots, and potting soil will intrigue the young horticulturist who may be housebound until spring.

Most of these unusual gifts imply some adult time at least to get started on projects. This time is the greatest gift you can give your child. Add some redeemable coupons to each kit–*"Good for one woodworking project;" "Good for one sewing activity"*––and watch your child's face light up.

D c. 26—Jan. 2

The week from December 26 to January 2 is a special time to be together for many families. With the holiday rush and excitement over, it is a time to relax and just enjoy the company of your child. If you are not going away, it is like a long, long weekend. In fact, you might consider some of the excursions mentioned in Chapter 2.

If the weather is bad or you are homebound for some other reason, you might want to try some of the following projects which make use of holiday leftovers. These are activities for you and your child to do together.

▶ Make a HOLIDAY COLLAGE. Gather pieces of wrapping paper, ribbon, tinsel, and cutout figures or scenes from greeting cards to create a collage. Encourage your child to tell you some of the special things he remembers from this holiday (who visited, what gifts he received, favorite songs sung, games played); all of which you can record on the back of the collage. Be sure to date the work of art and keep it safe as a holiday memory.

▶ Use old greeting cards to make SEWING CARDS for your child. Cut off the cover of a card and punch holes around the design in a simple way. Cut an 18-inch length of yarn and wrap one end in tape. Make a knot at the opposite end. Let your child "sew" through the holes.

▶ If you had turkey over the holidays, save the wishbone and help your child make a BOOKMARK with it. Scrub it clean and then paint it with acrylic paint. Cut an 18-inch length of grosgrain ribbon 1/2 inch wide and tie one end in a small bow. Tie the other end around the wishbone. Put the bookmark in your favorite holiday book.

▶ Don't forget to make TURKEY (chicken, beef, or whatever you have left over) SOUP with your child. Fill a large pot two-thirds full with broth and/or water and bring to a boil. Dump in bones and meat. Simmer one hour or more. Add chopped onion, diced potatoes, and any leftover vegetables. Simmer at least a half hour more. Your child can help you cut vegetables with a plastic knife, pour in broth and water, and, of course, stir the pot.

▶ POPCORN PICTURES provide a way to dispose of leftover snacks. Let your child glue the popcorn down onto paper to form a design, figure, or winter scene. You may wish to color the popcorn by dipping pieces into diluted food colors and drying them on paper towels. Have your child add details with a crayon or marker.

▶ Steal an evergreen branch from your holiday decorations and let your child create a WINTER WONDERLAND PICTURE. Place the branch on dark blue or green construction paper. Have your child dip an old toothbrush in white paint. Show him how to hold the brush in one hand and draw the thumb from the other hand across it over the paper. This will splatter paint on the paper. Have him continue until he sees the outline of the evergreen branch against a white background. Let the paint dry; then, give your child white glue to dab on the picture and glitter to sprinkle on the glue.

▶ If you don't save your gift boxes, give them to your child and challenge him to make an EMPTY BOX SCULPTURE. After gluing the boxes together, he can decorate them with paint, crayons, or markers.

TOGETHER

Don't throw out last year's calendar! Consider the ideas on the following page.

CALENDAR FUN

COLOR PATTERNS

YOU'LL NEED:

crayons or markers

old calendar pages

WHAT TO DO:

Child can fill in squares with colors to make designs or pictures.

CALENDAR TOSS

YOU'LL NEED:

flat pebbles   old calendar pages

WHAT TO DO:

Use old calendar pages and see if your child can toss a flat pebble onto a number or square and name the number (most children will say "2" and "5" for "25" which is fine.)

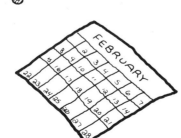

H ppy New Y r

New Year's Eve is traditionally NOT a celebration for children. But, whether you are having a party at home or going out, your child is definitely aware that something special is going on. If he is not allowed some kind of participation, he will feel left out. So why not plan a pint-sized New Year's Eve party, either early on the evening of December 31 or on January 1.

TOGETHER

Make New Year's favors with your child to enjoy at the party. Make funny hats using old wrapping paper, ribbon, and the directions on page 141.

▶   Have everyone in the family (and close friends, if you've invited some) contribute to a LAST YEAR MURAL. Spread out a large piece of paper and have each person draw something from the past year. This is a good way to reminisce over the "special times" you've had together—the camping weekend, the trip to the zoo, someone's birthday party, when everyone pitched in to paint the kitchen... Don't limit your art media—some people may want to create collages, cut out pictures from magazines, use paints or chalk. If your family is not the type to get down on the floor and all contribute to a mural (though this is part of the togetherness fun), give everyone their own sheet to draw on and then bind the results into a book.

▶   Play some favorite family games, perhaps some that you learned in the past year. Play charades and have everyone act out an experience the whole group has shared from the past year for the others to guess. Sing your favorite songs, especially those that evoke happy memories.

▶   Have your child help you bake a special THREE KING'S CAKE, a traditional dessert from Greece. Use your favorite cake recipe—letting your child measure, pour, break eggs, stir, and grease the pan—and add three whole almonds (large enough so you don't worry about a young child swallowing them) to the batter, before baking. Bake according to directions. Frost the cake with white frosting and decorate with quarters of red and green apples around the edge and any other decorations that make the cake look like a crown. As you eat the cake, the three people who find the almonds are the three kings. Have aluminum foil crowns prepared for them to wear for the rest of the party.

ALMOND

3 KINGS CAKE
(3 ALMONDS HIDDEN
IN BATTER)

NEW YEAR'S FAVORS

TIN PLATE RATTLERS

YOU'LL NEED:

tape

handful of dried beans

stapler

paper streamers

2 aluminum foil pie plates

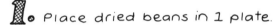
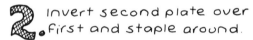
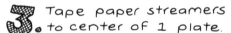

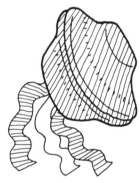

WHAT TO DO:

1. Place dried beans in 1 plate.

2. Invert second plate over first and staple around.

3. Tape paper streamers to center of 1 plate.

NOISEMAKER CRACKERS

YOU'LL NEED:

1 frozen orange juice can

tissue paper

curly ribbon

wrapped candy or trinkets

glue

scissors

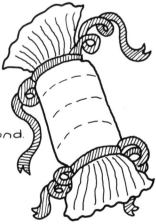

WHAT TO DO:

1. Remove both ends of orange juice can.

2. Measure tissue paper so it extends 3" beyond the 2 ends of the can and completely wraps around.

3. Glue tissue paper around can and tie 1 end with ribbon. Fringe with scissors.

4. Fill can with candy and close the open end with ribbon. Fringe that end.

Valentine's Day, Hurrah!

Just when winter is at its bleakest, along comes a holiday full of warmth. Valentine's Day is the perfect time to talk about feelings with your child and perhaps add to his emotional vocabulary.

This may be a good time for you to take a look at your own attitude towards emotions. Were you encouraged to share your feelings when you were young? Were the adults in your world interested in how you felt? Did other children understand and comfort you or tease you when you expressed your emotions?

If you learned to hide your emotions as a child, you'll remember that it wasn't a very pleasant experience. Now, it is important for you to ask yourself whether you are creating an atmosphere for your child where he feels safe to express his emotions, where he knows that his feelings will be respected.

If you hid your emotions in childhood, are you still hiding them today? Many of us feel it is wrong for adults to show (especially to their children) that they are sad, angry, and embarrassed or even happy, grateful, and loving. I feel that just the opposite is true. If we want our children to trust us with their feelings, we must trust them with ours.

Your child is learning to handle his feelings by watching you handle yours. When you are upset, it is important to acknowledge your feelings in words and to let your child know that he is not the cause (if he isn't). *"I am very upset because the oven isn't working and it is going to be hard to fix dinner. I am not angry with you."* If your child is the cause, be specific. *"It makes me angry when you leave your toys all over the house,"* NOT *"You're a bad boy!"*

Your goal is to have your child share his emotions freely and to be able to express why he feels the way he does. Sometimes young children do not have the vocabulary to express their feelings. They are overwhelmed by emotion and cannot find the words to describe them. That is why it is so important to talk about being happy, sad, upset, angry, joyful, embarrassed, and all the rest of the whole range of feelings with your child. When his behavior shows some strong emotion, ask him if he is happy, or sad, or if he feels good or bad. Accept whatever he says; there's nothing worse than hearing, *"That's silly. You can't be sad about that!"*

Valentine's Day gives your child lots of opportunities to talk about things that he loves. Also, encourage him to discuss things that he "likes" or things that are "okay," and things that he "doesn't like" or that are "yucky."

Sometimes words just won't express what your child is feeling. Give him the opportunity to play out feelings with dolls or stuffed animals or draw an angry monster on a piece of paper and then tear it up to get rid of angry feelings. It may just be important for you to be there--someone who knows, loves, and accepts him--in order for him to act out his feelings.

AN "I LOVE"... BOOK

My Favorite Things

YOU'LL NEED:

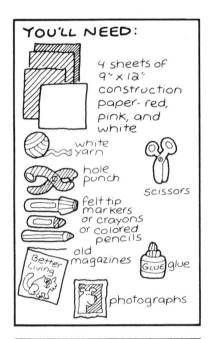

4 sheets of 9" x 12" construction paper- red, pink, and white

white yarn

hole punch

scissors

felt tip markers or crayons or colored pencils

old magazines

glue

photographs

WHAT TO DO:

1. Fold each piece of paper in half and trace a large heart onto it, making sure the left side of the heart overlaps the fold slightly. (see diagram.) →

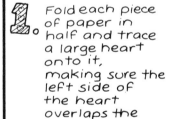

FOLD

9"

6"

2. Repeat with all 4 sheets of paper to create 8 pages. (2 heart pages per sheet.)

← 2 pages

3. Fold pages together. Punch holes and bind with yarn.

4. Draw or cut out and glue on pictures of favorite things. If possible, include photographs

My Favorite Things

Adult ↱ writes title

Valentine's Day Party

Mid-February is the perfect time for a party. Just a few friends and some HEART-warming activities make for a really special time.

▶ There is an easy way for children to make their own hearts. First, fold a piece of paper in half. Show each child how to hold the paper in one hand with his thumb over the fold slanting upward. Then, have him trace around his thumb with a pencil. Finally, have him remove his thumb and cut on the traced line while keeping the paper folded.

▶ Let children cut out a few of these hearts and also make flower and leaf shapes from tissue paper. They can use these to make "STAINED GLASS." Prepare pieces of wax paper, two per child, the size of standard construction paper. Premix some liquid starch and water. Let children brush the mixture onto a piece of wax paper. Have them arrange some of the hearts and flowers they have cut out onto the sticky paper. Then, help them place the second piece of wax paper on top. When everything is dry, you can hang this decoration up in a window or near a light source and it will look like stained glass. You can frame each child's project between two construction paper heart outlines and trim the excess wax paper.

▶ If you have a willow tree or any tree with long, thin, flexible branches, you can help children create NATURAL HEARTS with four branches and some thick elastic bands. These hearts are beautiful all year long. In advance, with your child, gather four 30-inch branches for each heart. If they are stiff, soak them in water overnight. Hold the thick parts of the branches in your hand and secure them tightly together with an elastic band. Gently, bend two branches to the left and two to the right to form the top rounded section of the heart. Gather the branches at the bottom to make a point. Place an elastic band tightly around the branches. Leave each heart alone for a few days to dry or set. Then, with your child or a group at the party, decorate each one. The children might want to weave yarn or ribbon through the branches. They might want to tie on red paper hearts, artificial flowers, bows, or other little decorations. These hearts can be hung on the wall and their decorations can change in different seasons.

TOGETHER

Make Heart Cookies with the children. They will enjoy these familiar flavors in special holiday shapes.

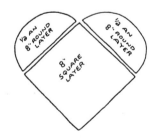

▶ What is a party without games? My favorite Valentine's Day game is a takeoff on Musical Chairs appropriately called "MUSICAL HEARTS." You'll need to make one large newsprint heart for each person playing. (This game works best with three to six people.) The paper hearts go on the floor and the children dance around them and listen for the music to stop. Each time it does, one heart is removed, BUT no one is out of the game. Now the children must share hearts when the music stops. The game is over when everyone is hugging to stay on the last heart. I love this game because there are NO losers–just the thing for Valentine's Day.

▶ If you've decided to make a heart-shaped cake for your celebration, there's no need to buy a special pan. One eight-inch square layer and one eight-inch round layer cut in half make a terrific heart shape. Place the two semi-circles on either side of one corner of the square and frost.

HEART COOKIES

YOU'LL NEED:

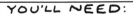

heart-shaped cookie cutters — ½ cup margarine — ¼ cup shortening — ¾ cup peanut butter — 1 cup sugar — 1 egg — 1 small jar raspberry jam

1 tsp. vanilla — 2 Tblsp. milk — 3 cups flour — rolling pin — cookie sheet — mixer — cooling rack — plastic knife

WHAT TO DO:

 1. Beat margarine, shortening, and peanut butter well. Add egg and beat well.

 2. Add sugar, vanilla, and flour with milk.

3. Chill 2 hours or more.

 4. Roll dough on lightly floured board to ¼" thick.

 5. Cut out heart shapes with cookie cutters.

 6. Place on a lightly greased cookie sheet. Bake at 350°F for 8–10 minutes (until slightly browned).

 7. Remove to cooling rack.

 8. Spread 1 tsp. jam on a cookie and cover with another for the peanut butter and jelly sandwich effect.

Spring Celebrations

TOGETHER

Use some of the Egg Shell Art ideas on the next page to make your eggs truly special. The wobbly egg can be Humpty Dumpty when you seat him on a sugar cube wall.

Whether you observe Easter or Passover, spring provides us with yet another excuse for a special celebration. Take some of the special time you spend with your child during the spring holidays to observe the changes in nature. Look at the branches on the trees, first for buds and then for leaves. If there is a pond nearby, look for frog eggs, then tadpoles, and finally frogs. Even if you live in a city, the grass in the park will turn green; there will be at least a few trees budding. Talk about how spring makes you feel. The change from gray and brown to green and yellow makes me feel great!

It is not surprising that the egg plays an important role in spring holidays. The egg has been recognized throughout history as a symbol of life. The ancient Egyptians began the tradition of coloring and exchanging gifts. Egg dying has remained a popular activity for this time of year. If you are ambitious, you can make this project into a science lesson for your child by creating your own natural dyes together. All you need is a small saucepan of water (to which you have added a pinch of salt) and one of the following: onion skins or saffron (yellow), coffee (brown), beets (red), red cabbage (purple), or blueberries (blue). Have your child help you chop or grind the basic ingredient you choose. Add it to the water in the saucepan and bring to a boil. Simmer for 20 minutes and strain. Dip hard-boiled or blown-out eggs (depending on whether you prefer egg salad or scrambled eggs with the leftovers) in the liquid dye.

If you are having a family gathering for Easter or Passover, your child might like to plant a few seeds in a styrofoam cup for each guest. He should do this a few weeks in advance of your celebration (planting a few extras in case some fail to grow). Then, he can place them in a sunny place (inside or out, depending on your weather) and observe their growth. Just before the big day, let your child decorate the cups with markers, stickers, and glitter. By adding the name of guest, you have created adorable place markers. If you are having an Easter party, your child may wish to make the delightful CAKE IN A BASKET on page 140.

Easter is a time for dressing up and showing off your finery. Dress up for play is an important learning activity for your child--male or female. It is a way for him to "try on" being an adult and perhaps to act out some of the problems he encounters dealing with the grown-up world. He may want to pretend to dress up for the Easter parade or Passover Seder before the fact. Make the FLOPPY HATS on page 141 with your child and add real spring materials like flowers, leaves, and seeds for trim. Talk about what "dressed up" means before the big day and let him help you decide what "he looks best in." The most important thing is that he feels good about the way he looks--that he feels good about himself. Sometimes, it is difficult for fashion-conscious parents to accept that their child is "looking his best" in old jeans and a t-shirt that was a gift from Grandpa; but, unless coat and tie or fancy dress is a must, try to accept that your child's good self-esteem will "dress up" any outfit.

EGG SHELL ART ooo

YOU'LL NEED:

colored tissue paper

liquid starch

glue water

elastic bands

egg dye or

food coloring

water

1 teaspoon vinegar

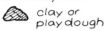

yarn

clay or play dough

markers oooo eggs

WHAT TO DO:

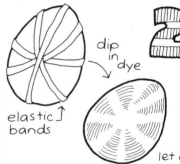

1. WOBBLY EGG HEADS

Remove insides of egg through ½" hole at the top. Squirt glue through the hole and poke a piece of clay or playdough to the bottom of the egg. Carefully draw a face on the shell. Cover hole with yarn. Push lightly and it wobbles!

dip in dye

elastic bands

let dry and remove elastic bands

2. STRIPED EGGS

Place elastic bands around shell of a hard boiled egg in any type of pattern. Dip egg into commercial or home-made egg dye (food coloring, warm water, 1 teaspoon vinegar). Let dry. Remove elastic bands.

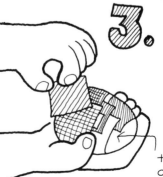

3. TISSUE PAPER EGGS

Dip torn pieces of colored tissue paper into liquid starch or diluted white glue and stick them onto an egg shell (of a blown-out egg). Overlap the tissue. Let dry for a bright, glossy egg.

tissue paper-
dipped into liquid starch or diluted white glue.

CAKE IN A BASKET

YOU'LL NEED:

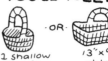

1 shallow 8" OR 9" round basket with handle · OR · 13" x 9" oblong basket

jelly beans

1 carrot or spice cake mix

empty jar

green food coloring

1 yd. ribbon

cooling rack

1 cup shredded coconut

OR baking pan - similar in size and shape to basket

white frosting of your choice

OR **MAKE YOUR OWN**
1. mix 6 oz. cream cheese
3 cups confectionary sugar
2 tsp. vanilla
2. Beat well.

WHAT TO DO:

1.
Bake the cake according to package directions. Make sure you bake it in a pan that will later enable it to fit into a basket.

2.
Remove cake from pan(s). Set on rack and put into freezer for 1-2 hours.

3.
Meanwhile, line basket with aluminum foil.

4.
Place frozen cake into foil-lined basket. You may have to cut 13" x 9" cake in half for it to fit into basket easier.

5.
Frost cake. Shake coconut with a few drops of green food coloring in a jar. Place this "grass" on top of frosting.

6.
Hide the jelly bean "eggs" in the "grass." Tie a ribbon on the handle.

FLOPPY HATS

YOU'LL NEED:

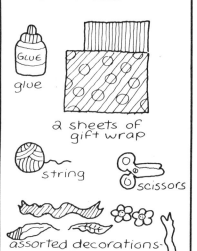

- glue
- 2 sheets of gift wrap
- string
- scissors
- assorted decorations - ribbon, flowers, feathers

WHAT TO DO:

1. Spread glue all over back side of 1 sheet of wrapping paper.

2. Place second sheet on top so that pretty sides are showing on top and bottom.

3. Place glued sheets on head and press down over head like a hat.

4. Secure with strings wrapped around in headband fashion.

5. Let set on head for 10 minutes. Remove and let it dry thoroughly.

6. Trim brim to a round shape. Add flowers, ribbons, feathers....

Patriotic Summer Holidays

Memorial Day and the Fourth of July are times for celebration—and just enjoying the outdoors. Let your child help you plan the backyard barbecue or family picnic.

If you have even a few children at your celebration, you can organize an impromptu parade. Use any rhythm instruments you have handy, but also add some drums, cymbals, and horns made with everyday household items. This is an excellent opportunity for children to brainstorm and use their creative thinking skills. Start with everyone in the kitchen and ask, *"What can we use for a drum?"* You may want to save some paper towel and toilet paper rolls in advance and ask, *"What sounds could we make with these?"* Move into other areas when you need more ideas.

You might want to include a large "HOMEMADE" AMERICAN FLAG in your parade. This is a perfect patriotic party project because it is made up of many activities: cutting, gluing, painting, measuring, drawing—the older children or adults can supervise the young ones—and, there is something for everyone to do. First, you'll need to have a cardboard tube from a roll of wrapping paper. Arrange four pieces of fingerpaint paper (or white shelving paper) into a rectangle with the longest side as long as the cardboard tube. (You can use pieces of construction paper that match the colors of the flag if you want to avoid the mess.) Tape the pieces together, using masking tape only on one side.

Cut seven pieces of red crepe paper streamers the length of the longest side of your rectangle. Glue them horizontally to make the stripes on your flag.

Have a young child fingerpaint a piece of paper blue. Have someone cut it into a perfect square to become the blue field of your flag. Glue the square to the upper lefthand corner of the large rectangle.

TOGETHER

When you are discussing fireworks, help your child make his own Fireworks Painting to display during the fireworks.

Trace or draw stars on white paper and have some of the children cut them out and glue them to the blue paper.

Roll the top of the flag around the wrapping paper tube and secure with masking tape. This flag can be carried in your parade by two children or it can decorate your front porch.

Before the holiday, discuss fireworks with your child. Has he ever heard and seen them? What did they look like? What did they sound like? Be sure to stay with him while watching fireworks. Some children are frightened by loud noises, others are not--and reactions may vary from year to year. So stay close in case your child needs a friendly lap.

FIREWORKS PAINTINGS

YOU'LL NEED:

 glue

 paper cups

 glitter

 black construction paper

  drinking straw

 plastic spoon

 water

  tempera paint- 3 bright colors

WHAT TO DO:

1. For each color, mix:

2 parts paint
1 part glue
2 drops water.

Put each mixture into a paper cup.

2. Put a spoonful of each color on a piece of black construction paper and blow through a straw directly over paint.

3. While paint is still wet, sprinkle on a little bit of glitter.

PARTIES 6

Let's Have a Party

Most of us think of children's parties as a way of showing our children a good time and also of demonstrating how much we love them. But, we rarely think of parties as learning experiences for our children.

From the invitation list to the final cleanup, the best party you can give involves your child as much as possible. Most children are already experienced party-givers by the time they are three—teas for their stuffed animals, luncheons for dolls, play picnics in the backyard with a friend.

While working on all aspects of a party, your child will be practicing skills she will need later in school and in life. The chart on the next page will give you an idea of the many pre-reading skills she will use while preparing for and then attending her own party.

When her birthday approaches, ask your child what kind of party she would like. Young children are not into major themes, but she might have attended one of her friend's that she particularly liked or heard about one that sounded fun. This chapter presents some easy themes and ideas that you might want to suggest. Remember to keep the emphasis of the party where it belongs—on your child, her friends, the foods she enjoys, the activities she likes to do. Often, well-meaning parents get caught in the trap of trying to plan a party they think their child will enjoy, one that is just like or "bigger and better" than their next-door neighbor's was last month. What sounds good to you or what impresses other parents is probably not your child's idea of the perfect party.

Surprise parties are NOT for young children. Another reason to let your child help you plan the party is that in this way she will know what to expect. She will not build up false expectations that could ruin the big day. Knowing what is coming will make her feel more comfortable and secure when the time comes. Many a preschooler has spent her whole birthday party alone in her room, overwhelmed by the festivities outside. Be sure to read The Berenstain Bears and Too Much Birthday by Stan and Jan Berenstain together before the party. It will give you both some wise thoughts on planning and also give your child some idea of what to expect in terms of the party itself and her feelings.

Let your child make up the guest list. That wise old saying, "Invite your child's age plus one," still holds true, but you may have a very social four-year-old who wants to invite ten friends. Unless space or the logistics of a trip (to a movie or the zoo) is a problem, try to accede to your child's wishes. But, DON'T invite your child's whole class because you feel you should or the whole neighborhood even though your child only plays with three other children who live nearby. Encourage your child to help you with the invitations. It's an excellent opportunity for her to deal with the questions "What," "Where," "When," and "Who" in a concrete situation.

	Recalling Details	Sequence	Following Directions	Predicting	Cause and Effect	Comparing	Classifying	Main Idea	Drawing Conclusions	Generalizing	Picture Interpretation	Realism or Fantasy
1. Decide to have a party.								X	X			
a. Talk about favorite ones.	X					X	X					
b. Talk about special times that can be celebrated.										X		
2. Decide what kind of party to have.				X			X	X				
3. Decide what to do to get ready for party.		X										
a. Make lists.		X	X									
b. Plan schedule.		X	X									
4. Decide who to invite.									X			
5. Write and/or decorate the invitations.			X									
6. Choose menu.							X					
a. Recall favorite foods.	X											
b. Pick out certain foods for special days.							X					
7. Shop for food.							X					
8. Decorate room and/or table.			X									
a. Pick or make flowers.			X									
b. Make placemats.			X								X	
c. Choose dishes.							X					
9. Prepare food.		X										
10. Set table.		X	X									
11. Entertain guests.			X									
a. Choose games.							X					
b. Tell favorite stories.	X											X
c. Put on plays or puppet shows.			X									X

Ideas for Parties

Let your child help you decide on the menu and then go shopping with you for the food. Discuss important matters, such as how many hamburger buns you will need, whether you should buy large or individual bags of potato chips. In the store, let her count the number of buns in a package. *"If there are six buns in a package, how many packages will we need to buy for eight children?"* Let her estimate how many large bags of potato chips will be needed for eight children. Planning a menu can be an important math lesson!

TOGETHER

Your child can help make these easy and festive Party Decorations.

If decorations are needed, let your child help you plan and make them. Crepe paper streamers and balloons in your child's favorite colors are really all you need. If you don't have a theme, continue the color scheme at the table with paper plates, cups, and napkins. A favorite stuffed animal holding a bunch of balloons makes a very effective centerpiece.

Talk about games. Find out which ones your child enjoys at school and at other parties. You might check with her teacher for suggestions. You'll find the rules to the old favorites (and some new ones, too) in <u>Games for Children</u> by Marguerite Kohl and Frederica Young and <u>Games (And How to Play Them)</u> by Anne Rockwell. Don't forget to sit in a circle and sing some favorite songs, too. These, and perhaps a story—chosen by the birthday child—read aloud may work better than organized games. Really young children are not used to large group activities and may prefer playing with toys in small groups rather than participating in party games where they have to learn new rules. Don't force anyone to join in; and if no one shows any interest in a planned activity, go on to something else.

Young children do not need or expect prizes when they play a game. Unless everyone can win, prizes take away from the fun of the game. Try to find noncompetitive games or add a new twist to competitive ones like the variation of "Musical Chairs" on page 136.

Your child will probably change her mind a hundred times before the party. Make lots of lists together and check them regularly. There are so many opportunities for learning when your child takes responsibility for her own party. Just think! She is getting learning experiences in:

- Remembering other fun parties, games, songs
- Organizing and planning invitations, menu, games, decorations
- Being considerate of others
- Making things--decorations, invitations, food
- Reading names, labels
- Writing lists, invitations
- Spending money at the supermarket or party store
- And so much more!

TOGETHER

PARTY DECORATIONS

WHAT TO DO:

TABLECLOTH

Use a large piece of tissue paper or wrapping paper or an old, clean sheet. Cover tablecloth with crayon or marker drawings. This idea may be adapted for any occasion.

For variety: drape crepe paper streamer around sides of tablecloth.

PLACEMATS AND NAPKIN RINGS

For placemats - draw pictures relating to holiday or special occasion on construction paper. Adult covers art work with clear contact paper.

For napkin rings - cut cardboard tubes to 2". Wrap tissue paper around each and decorate with markers.

CENTERPIECES

Fold small pieces of colored cardboard in half for a stand. Glue on child's drawing

OR

Prop up child-made puppet on cardboard tube.

OR

Make a mobile centerpiece - cut out child's drawings and suspend from drinking straw.

A Teddy Bear Tea

On my daughter's fourth birthday, we celebrated with a teddy bear tea party. We bought invitations with bear stickers on them, but if you and your child are feeling creative, you can have her trace a teddy shape onto brown construction paper and cut out her own invitations. Print your message and then duplicate enough copies to paste one on each paper bear. Be sure to invite the children AND their favorite stuffed bear.

I invited the children to come from 1:30 to 4:00 on a Sunday afternoon. Two and one-half hours is the maximum time I would plan for a preschool party, less for younger children or if the children cannot go outside to play.

When the guests arrived, I gave them headbands I had cut from brown construction paper with semi-circles for ears stapled on. They decorated these with stickers and markers, and then I stapled the bands around their heads, so everyone looked like a party bear.

Then, two at a time, I invited the children into the kitchen to make bear cookies. I had made the simple sugar cookie dough in advance with my daughter, so that all her guests had to do was to cut out a teddy with a cookie cutter, place it on a prelabeled square of tin foil, and decorate it with raisins, sprinkles, and candy bits. While the children were playing games, we baked the cookies and then served them at "teatime."

We played "The Farmer in the Dell," "Duck, Duck, Goose," "London Bridge," and "Follow the Leader"–all favorites at my daughter's nursery school and chosen by her in advance. Then, we had a teddy bear parade (to the music of "Teddy Bear Picnic") and a contest to judge the children's stuffed animals. Everyone got a prize–the largest, smallest, funniest, best-dressed–it was easy to find a category to fit each contestant.

Then, it was time for our birthday tea party. I served root beer instead of tea, but used real tea cups so everyone felt very grown-up. We had tiny tea sandwiches of peanut butter and/or honey. (My daughter loves the combination. Ugh!) Finally, we had ice cream cake in the shape of a teddy bear and the cookies each child had baked.

After tea, we played "Pin the Tie on the Teddy" using an inexpensive poster and bowties made of ribbon. We laughed over the funny places the bowties ended up and everyone had such fun that a prize was unnecessary.

I think all the children had a good time and my husband, the veteran of many, many such parties with my stepsons, pronounced it a success. I must admit, however, that the only person who was a little disappointed was my daughter, who, the day before the party–after weeks of helping me plan and prepare–had announced that she wanted to have a Rainbow Brite party. Well, the best-laid plans...

Film Festival

This is an easy and excellent INDOOR party. Your invitations can resemble theater tickets. If you don't own a video cassette recorder, you can rent or borrow one. Let your child choose a full-length children's movie to show at the party. It's not easy, but try to find one without scary parts for the more squeamish members of the audience. For a very young group, I suggest a tape with a few short fairy tales or familiar stories. (Curious George is one of our favorites.) You can plan for a number of intermissions—with a short game or song during each. Provide lots of popcorn and juice in festive paper cups—and you can sit back, relax, and enjoy the movie.

Treasure Hunt

Children love treasure hunts. The words *treasure* and *pirate* make all of us feel adventurous. But, if you are having more than three or four guests, this party works well ONLY if you can use the OUTDOORS.

In advance, fill shoeboxes, one for each guest, with small surprises and treats. Make sure that food treats are tightly wrapped to avoid being eaten or disturbed by insects. Write each child's name on her treasure box.

Before the guests arrive, hide the boxes. As each child arrives, give her directions to finding her special treasure. You can give the directions orally, *"Your treasure is on top of something black that holds water"* (a bucket). If you don't have too many children, you can draw a treasure map for each one. You can cut pictures of familiar landmarks (swing, furniture, tree) out of magazines.

If the party is outside and you have access to a sandbox, you might hide some small plastic animals in the sand and have children, one or two at a time, "dig for treasure." Make sure each child takes only one animal.

Provide children with bandannas to wear "pirate-style" as party hats. For refreshments, have cupcakes into which you have "buried" a candy treat before baking. Your child will enjoy helping you make these in advance.

To calm everybody down at the end of the party or right before refreshments, have your little pirates sit in a circle. Read them a book chosen by your child.

INSIDE THE SANDBOX...

Buried Treasures

Pasta Party

color
pattern
bracelet

cardboard

If your child's favorite food is *"s'getti,"* she would probably enjoy a party with a slightly Italian flavor. Provide a wholesome, filling lunch, cooking up batches of pasta in a variety of flavors and shapes. Put them out in bowls and let children take a little of each before you add the sauce. (Some children prefer their pasta plain.)

After lunch, let the children make MACARONI JEWELRY. Before the party, use diluted food color to dye uncooked macaroni–ziti, elbows, wagon wheels, for example. Place one type (or a mixture) in a plastic bag with a little water and food coloring. Seal the bag and let your child shake it to coat the pasta with color. Together you can lay the macaroni on paper towels. This is a wonderful pre-party activity for you and your child to do together. You can even decorate the birthday cake with colored noodles.

Provide all of the guests with string or yarn, knotted at one end with a cardboard scrap to keep the noodles from slipping off. Let them create color and shape patterns. Patterning is a very important thinking skill for children. They have to observe what came before and then predict what comes next. Encourage very young children to make either a shape OR a color pattern necklace. Older children can combine the two concepts to make more complicated patterns.

Arts and Crafts Celebration

Let children make their own party favors and the process will become the main event at your child's party. On the invitation, be sure to indicate that guests should wear play clothes, since craft projects can get very messy. Also, you can ask for a contribution such as an egg carton, oatmeal box, or old, holey socks.

Review your child's favorite projects brought home from school or look at the TOGETHER activities in this book for inspiration. Choose a project that the children can complete almost independently. Remember that the process is much more important than the product; the "doing" is the fun part. The object is to keep the children busy at the party and to give them something to take home as a memento of a good time. At the end of the party, you can have an art show for the parents of the guests.

TOGETHER

Plan a Clown Party with your child. She can help you with the decorations, food, and activities.

CLOWN PARTY

1. PAPER PLATE CLOWN

← yarn

balloon nose

marker

FRONT VIEW

paper plate

SIDE VIEW

balloon nose

2. CLOWN POSTER

CLOWNS

Use colored construction paper and wet, colored chalk.

3. CLOWN MAKE-UP

Use lipstick, blush-on, and eye shadow applied with clean cotton swabs or make GREASE PAINT.

2 Tblsp. white shortening

2 Tblsp. cornstarch

1 tsp. flour

Color with cocoa or food colors.

4. CLOWN TRAIN

Make a train from large boxes and paper plates.

5. CLOWN SANDWICHES

cut-out bread slices spread with peanut butter

raisins

strawberry jelly

raisins

shredded coconut

6. CLOWN FACE PIÑATA

Cover a large balloon with strips of newspaper dipped into a thick mixture of wallpaper paste and water. Let dry. Glue on tissue paper hair and paint on a face. Pop the balloon. Fill with candy and toys

Birthdays in School

Practically all young children celebrate their birthdays in school. Even if your child was born in August, she deserves that special time of recognition by her classmates each year.

Schools have different policies on birthdays. In some classrooms, there is a monthly celebration, acknowledging everyone whose birthday falls in that month. If this is the policy in your child's school, you may be asked to contribute a special party treat or decoration to be part of the collective celebration. Be sure that you know the exact number of children in the group if you are bringing in individual goodies--and always add one or two extras for emergencies.

If your school celebrates each child's birthday separately, you can probably be more creative in your participation. If you are tired of baking cupcakes, try a put-together snack, like APPLES FROM OUTER SPACE--it's as fun to make as it is to eat. Put a small apple, some small cheese cubes, and pretzel sticks in a zip locking bag, one for each child in the group. Have some forks on the table during snacktime, so that the children can poke holes in the apples. Then, they can push the pretzel sticks into the holes and put the cheese cubes on the ends of the pretzels. The children will compare their wacky creations and then gobble them up.

TOGETHER

With your child, assemble the parts of these Melon Boats in zip-locking bags to take to school for a birthday snack.

With the cooperation of her teacher, you might want to find a special game to teach the children on your child's birthday. Bring along a small treat for snack, but make the game the main event. For creative games, try The Party Book for Boys and Girls by Bernice Carlson, The Golden Happy Birthday Book compiled by Barbara Shook Hazen, and Confetti by Phyllis Fiarotta and Noel Fiarotta.

If the idea of playing games with 26 four-year-olds doesn't appeal to you, perhaps reading to them does. Why not buy a book and present it to the school in your child's name on her birthday? This is a really nice way to build up the class library and your child will feel terrific every time she takes it off the shelf and sees her name inscribed inside. Maybe her teacher will let you read it to the class at circletime on her birthday. Let your child choose the book you will donate. If she doesn't have a favorite, you might want to find one on the subject of birthdays, like Spot's Birthday Party by Eric Hill, The Birthday Party by Helen Oxenbury, or Happy Birthday to Me by Anne and Harlow Rockwell. (Of course, check to make sure that the class doesn't already have the book you have chosen.)

MELON BOAT

YOU'LL NEED:

 blueberries -or-
strawberries -or-
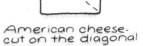 grapes

toothpicks

 long, thick pretzel

American cheese - cut on the diagonal

 1 melon wedge

WHAT TO DO:

 1. Make a "mast" in melon wedge with a long, thick pretzel.

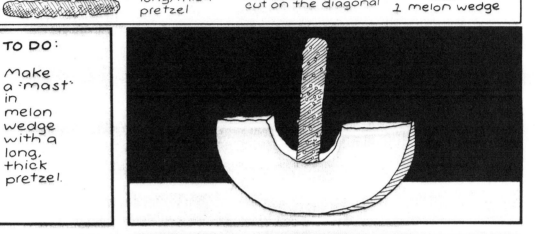

 **2.** Add cheese "sails". Secure with toothpicks.

LIKE THIS   OR THIS

 3. Make "sailors" with fruit slipped onto toothpicks.

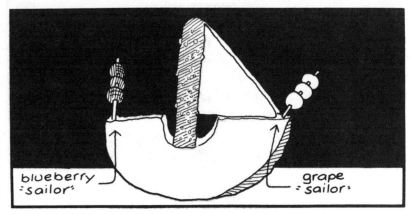

blueberry "sailor"

grape "sailor"

TIMES OF STRESS 7

Dealing with Stress

Childcare Stresses

Choosing Childcare

Changing Schools

Moving Days

Coping with Divorce

Illness

Encounters with Death

Siblings

Dealing with Stress

Our children—we, also—are in the process of becoming. That entails good times and bad ones, times of great joy and times of stress. And, when times of stress are upon us, the thing which saves us is the feeling that we are loved.

A good self-image is the most important factor in your child's makeup when it comes to dealing with stress. Throughout this book, I have tried to give you ways to promote your child's self-esteem in almost everything you do together. However, even the child who feels terrific about himself will need additional support and understanding when he is faced with situations like family quarrels and economic difficulties, Mother going back to work, divorce, remarriage, moving, new schools, illness, and death.

Your young child has probably not developed the verbal, emotional, and intellectual skills to state his feelings as well as an adult. This means that you have to pick up his distress signals and understand what he is trying to express. Sometimes, we have to redefine the term "misbehavior." Crying, refusal to eat or go to sleep, and aggressive behavior may not be the manifestations of a spoiled brat, but rather cries for help from a troubled child. Look for changes in behavior—patterns of sleeping, eating, going to the bathroom—as signals that your child needs help. An outgoing child may suddenly be withdrawn or a shy, quiet child may become very aggressive. Also, your child's normal behavior may become exaggerated—less controlled, communicative, or cooperative. You know your child better than anyone, so the responsibility for listening, observing, and interpreting rests with you.

Sometimes, changes in your child's behavior are due to developmental growth. Acting out and testing are part of every new stage. They are the means by which your child defines the boundaries of his world. You can read about these stages and what to expect in books, but I have found that these are less helpful than the feedback of other parents and my child's teachers. In general, trust your own instincts. When you feel your child is overstressed—and it may be for a variety of seemingly unrelated and uneventful circumstances, not one major problem like divorce—it's time for you to step in and lend some support.

Everyday Stresses

Young children are creative copers. They find ingenious ways to deal with everyday stresses. In the process of his development, your child will learn to cope with many, many problems, situations, fears, and people that he finds uncomfortable. From these big and little crises, your child learns values, develops the ability to choose between alternatives, and builds the faith that problems can, and will, be solved. Stressful situations are an important part of his education. Coping with problems helps to build self-esteem.

Observing and listening to the way your child works out the solutions to problems for himself will help you understand the level on which he is ready to act. Sometimes, we expect our children to be more mature than they are able. Other times, we don't give them enough credit and step in when it isn't necessary.

If your child is just having a rough day and can't seem to cope, here are some useful techniques from Kathleen Koons to relieve the tension.

▶ Deep breathing is a technique that works well in any situation where a person is feeling fear or stress. Encourage your child to try this by suggesting that he pretend that he is blowing up a giant balloon. With each deep breath he takes and then lets out, the balloon gets bigger. Talk him through the situation. Finally, the balloon bursts and he collapses to the floor. This deep breathing exercise along with a change in activity will help most children wind down.

▶ Progressive relaxation is another technique that your child can benefit from. Tell him to be a soldier at attention with his body stiff and hands glued to his sides. Then, suddenly tell him to be a rag doll—all parts of his body have become loose and floppy. Or, he can be a robot and walk around with stiff movements; suddenly he becomes an astronaut floating weightlessly in space.

▶ Your child can relax with soothing mental images, too. When his mind is clear, he is better able to solve problems and have original ideas. Tell or read him stories that encourage peacefulness and quiet. Make up stories about floating clouds, falling leaves, sleepy puppies, anything he can focus on that suggests calm. Let him pretend to be that cloud or leaf or perhaps a falling snowflake or a slow-moving turtle.

Calming Activities

Early Childhood teachers know which activities in the classroom can be used to help a child who is angry, wound up, depressed, or fearful. In the same way, you can direct your child to certain activities at home to reduce stress and to diffuse unhappy feelings.

Waterplay is a very calming activity if you notice that your child is wound up. Playing in the sink with a few plastic containers and some soapy water works well and is especially useful in the early evening as you cook dinner and your child is tired and cranky.

Art projects can help your child when he is stressed. Fingerpainting can have a calming effect as can working with play dough. He can also use art projects to work through problems. Your child has control over his project so he can create whatever he likes—and destroy it. He can draw a picture that portrays his family as he would like it to be if he feels sad that Daddy doesn't live at home any more. If he is afraid of monsters in his closet, he can draw them and then tear up the picture. The process is even more therapeutic if you can get him to discuss his feelings as he is working. Remember to accept those feelings—whatever they are—feelings are never "wrong."

In the same way that "music soothes the savage beast," it can calm your child. Most children are sensitive to the moods that music creates. When your child is stressed, choose lullabies and classical selections for background music as he plays. Dancing to upbeat music can be an effective way to release tension.

Music plays an important role in many Early Childhood classrooms to ease transitions and change moods. The housekeeping/dramatic play area is another tool teachers use to help a troubled child work out problems. Similarly, you can encourage your child to dress up and act out his problems with his toys. Sometimes, you can set the stage with props, and other times, you can suggest an actual game. Your child can take out his anger at feeling displaced with a "baby" doll. He can play the role of doctor to his stuffed animals or teacher with you as student to work out problems at school.

There have been many books written for young children on subjects like death, divorce, hospital stays, and other stressful situations. Often, when you read with your child about the problems of a third party, your child can talk about his own feelings with greater ease. I have placed the titles of pertinent books throughout this chapter. A children's librarian can direct you to others.

Often, when your child is under stress, he will take his books and perhaps a few dearly loved stuffed animals or a blanket and go off by himself. This is one way of coping we all use. It's important that your child has a place he can go to and feel secure and comfortable--a place of his own. A large carton fixed up attractively with pillows, perhaps a tape recorder and some favorite tapes, even some pretty, sweet-smelling flowers you place there on strategic days, is enough to give him that needed refuge.

All of these activities suppose that you are in touch with the fact that your child is under some stress. Remember when you notice symptoms that the causes may not be immediately apparent. But, if your child feels that you care in his time of need, he will eventually open up and you can help him solve his problems--or at least understand them.

A QUIET PLACE

Inside a large carton or in a corner....

stuffed animal

picture or photograph

books

big pillows

A FELT BOARD (or chalk board)

DRAWING MATERIALS: paper, crayons, clipboard

← piece of carpet or small area rug

Childcare Stress

When your child goes to school or a daycare center for the first time, you will both suffer the stress of separation. For so many parents today, the question is not whether to send their young children into a childcare situation, but rather which one. By 1990, about 70% of mothers with children under six will be in the work force on a fulltime basis.

If you have been on leave from your job or have decided to start working outside the home, the change, itself, can be stressful to your child. Don't suddenly disappear one day for eight hours. Make the transition gradually, going away for a few hours at a time at first. Show your child where you are going to work and, if possible, take him inside to see what you do. If you work in an office, bring home some supplies and encourage your child to play office at home. Through observing his play, you may find that he has some misconceptions about what you do that are easily correctable. Sonya's Mommy Works text and photographs by Arlene Alda and First Pink Light by Eloise Greenfield and Moneta Barnett—a book about a father being away and then returning—are good books to share with your child on this subject.

This situation can create a lot of stress for you, too. I, for one, am upset by the guilt promoted by some Early Childhood experts who claim that mothers should stay home with their children fulltime at least until the age of three. To my mind, the energy you expend on guilt would be better used seeking out the best possible childcare for your child.

Choosing Childcare

Even if you are available to take care of your child on a fulltime basis, you will probably want him to start spending time with groups of children his own age during his preschool years. This is very healthy. The most important job you have is to find the right program, a place where you feel your child will receive the same kind of care and attention he would get at home. Find out if your community has a childcare network—a clearing house for all the childcare programs in your area. You may be able to choose between a babysitter, a family daycare home—where one adult takes care of a small group of children in her home—a daycare center, a nursery school, or, if you are lucky, an onsite corporate childcare center at your place of work.

Once you have found a place or places that offer hours which work into your schedule and are accessible to your home or workplace, the next step is to pay a visit. Before you go, you will want to be clear on your goals for your child in this program. If it is a toddler playgroup, perhaps you want him to learn to socialize with other children and to become comfortable in the care of an adult other than yourself. If he is entering a pre-kindergarten program, you may want him to be developing concepts and skills, as well as socializing and learning to follow classroom rules and routines.

Talk with the director, some of the teachers, and, perhaps, some of the other parents about the school's child development philosophies and attitudes towards children in general. To me, it is most important that my child is in a place where the caregivers respect young children and will work towards developing their self-esteem and creativity. I want an environment that nurtures the whole child—the physical, intellectual, social, and emotional sides of him. **And,** I want a place where I will feel comfortable about visiting during the year and sharing ideas with my child's teachers.

When your visit the school for the first time, look at the arrangement of the room and the materials available for play. Here are some guidelines.

▶ Is the classroom cheerful and organized so that play areas and learning centers are inviting to children?

▶ Are the toys well kept? Which ones are out for children to choose?

▶ Are the walls covered with colorful, stimulating pictures?

▶ Do the following areas exist in the classroom: block area, water table, art center, cooking area, library corner, housekeeping/dramatic play area, nature/science table or bulletin board, music area? These are not all necessarily out at the same time. However, if you don't see anything to do with music, for example, in the room, you should ask how it fits into the curriculum.

▶ What is the daily schedule like? Find out how the day is divided for the children. Are there quiet and active times? Is there a story time everyday? Is there a snack? If the children are there for a long time, is there a rest period?

At my child's school, there is a daily schedule for parents and children to read together when they arrive in the morning. This allows me to ask specific questions, instead of the usually fruitless *What did you do in school today?"* Newsletters can also keep parents informed on the activities at school.

▶ Find out the teacher/child ratio.

▶ Find out how medical emergencies are taken care of. Is there a nurse or emergency medical technician on the premises?

▶ Of course, find out if the childcare facility is licensed by the state. Even though each state has different regulations, the most important health and safety regulations nationally are fairly standard.

Most importantly, ask yourself whether this is a place you would like to spend time regularly if you were a child. If you cannot picture your child being happy in this setting, then you will not be able to give him the sense of confidence he needs to approach the experience positively. Also, you will probably never be truly relaxed or able to concentrate on your own work while he is there and he will sense this.

Once you choose a school or daycare program, there are a few things you can do to make those first few days at school easier for your child and his teacher. These suggestions come from veteran teachers Jeannine Perez, Nancy McKeever, and Mary Beth Spann.

▶ Plan your child's school wardrobe carefully. Keep his small motor skill development in mind—velcro, large buttons, and elastic waistbands are easy for small hands to handle. Properly-sized shoes and boots should be easy for your child to get on and off.

▶ Let your child help decide what he is going to wear to school. Let him decide what crayons, paper, and other materials to bring. When he has some control over the experience, he will feel that in some way he has been involved in the actual decision to go to school.

▶ The first day or few days, allow your child to bring something from home that makes him feel comfortable and secure: a stuffed animal, blanket, favorite book. Make sure he recognizes all of his belongings and that they are identified with his name.

▶ It is helpful for children to visualize things. Tell him what you will be doing while he is in school. Also, give him an idea of his own schedule. *"First, you will do fingerpainting, then you will read a story, then you will have snack, then you will play outside, and then I will be there to pick you up."*

▶ The very best thing you can give your child is encouragement and confidence. The hug and kiss when your child leaves you, notes from you to hang in his cubby help make the whole experience a success. When you show interest at the end of the day, your child can share those special times you haven't had together.

Go through the work your child brings home with him. Don't comment on the stars or checks, but ask him to explain "all of the hard work" to you. Put your child in the role of teacher and he will often feel more like discussing what he did in school. In this way, you can see which concepts your child has learned and which ones he still needs to develop. As for the many pieces of artwork that arrive home, look at each one with your child and ask him to tell you about it. Statements like, *"That's a lovely horse,"* can really upset your child when he is showing you his picture of a dog. Be nonjudgmental and always offer a note of encouragement like, *"I like the way you mixed those colors,"* or *"These shapes form such an interesting pattern."* Pictures may also be labeled with your child's words. Be sure to read them aloud; these are your child's first efforts at creative writing.

Changing Schools

Moving from one school to another—a necessity for most children at the age of four or five—can be very upsetting for your child when he is happy and secure in his present situation. Many young children are not receptive to change and it is especially difficult when your child has built up a special relationship with his teacher—often the same person for his whole preschool experience—and where he has learned routines and is safe and comfortable in the building and in his classroom.

If your child has older siblings, he may be looking forward to going to school with "the big kids." But, it may be harder for only children or the eldest child in the family. Here are some suggestions for easing the transition from Dr. Sally Bing.

▶ Children feel most secure when they have a regular routine, so try to arrange things so that your child can make the move in small steps. Talk about the new school occasionally, but don't discuss it to death. Be sensitive if your child clams up or looks pained every time you bring up the subject.

▶ Drive past the building so that your child knows what it looks like. If possible, arrange a short visit for both of you to his new classroom in the spring if your child is starting in the fall. Most teachers and school administrators don't mind these visits as long as you don't upset their routine.

▶ Before the end of the school year, get a list of the children in your neighborhood who will be in your child's class in the fall. You may wish to call several of the other parents and organize a small playgroup or arrange visits among two or more children at a time so they can become comfortable playing together.

▶ You might even consider setting up a summer "play school," where the children could practice skills like cutting, pasting, and painting. In this way, your child not only becomes acquanted with his future classmates, but also with some of the activities at his new school. Don't go overboard—a few days over a period of two weeks is more than enough unless all the children are clamoring for more. Also, remember that the emphasis is on fun—not academics!

▶ During the summer, go to the school playground with your child several times. Play games and try out the equipment if it has been left out. Let your child feel comfortable with his new setting. Late in August, you might even meet some of the teachers coming into school to organize their classrooms or for meetings. A few days before the beginning of the school year, discuss with your child his new routine. Tell him how he will be going to school, how long he will be there, and how he will be getting home. If he is taking the bus for the first time, you may wish to take a dry run with him before the first day. Assure him that each day he will walk with someone to the bus stop and someone will meet him there after school. For the first few days at least, you go with him and make sure he feels comfortable with the trip.

On the first day of school, follow through with what you have told your child. If he is upset and doesn't want you to leave, reassure him that you will meet him after school and let the teacher take over. It may take a little while, but once he sees the friends he made over the summer, does familiar activities, and goes out to play in a familiar playground, he will feel right at home.

Moving Days

We are living in a very mobile society. Many people move several times during their childhood years. There is a sense of loss and separation involved in any type of move—whether it is across the street, to a different city, to a new family, or across the world. All moves are important events, full of difficult adjustments for parents and children alike. But, in the long run, they can lead to growth. Here are some ideas from Jean Stangl to make the transition smoother and more comfortable for your child.

▶ If possible, take your child to visit the new home. If your new home is far away, show your child pictures of the house, his room, the backyard, the local park, his new school, and other landmarks. Any local Chamber of Commerce will send you a packet about its community free of charge.

▶ Discuss with your child why you are moving, how long the move will take, how you will travel to get there, and any exciting details you might have about his new home. Answer his questions as fully and honestly as you can. Your child may have unpleasant fantasies about why you are moving and what will happen when you arrive that you need to dispel as soon as you can.

▶ As moving day approaches, help your child deal with his anticipation by letting him mark off the days on a calendar or making an Advent-style calendar like the one on page 115, using a large house instead of a tree shape and furniture instead of holiday ornaments.

▶ Encourage your child to help decide what to pack and how to decorate his new room. At quiet times—and you should plan for some—during the move, read some stories together about moving and about new homes. Look for the following at your local library. And, of course, pay a visit with your child to your new library as soon as you are settled.

- The Big Hello by Janet Schulman
- The House on 88th Street by Bernard Waber
- I'm Moving by Martha Hickman
- Janey by Charlotte Zolotow
- Moving Away by Alice Viklund
- The New Boy by Mary Lystad
- Will You Be My Friend? by Chihiro Iwasaki

▶ If you are moving nearby, think about having a party for old friends as soon as you are settled. Or, you might have a "get acquainted" party to introduce your child to people in the new neighborhood. Try to invite as many children as possible.

Moving is a stressful experience for everyone in the family. Be open with your child about your own feelings. There will be times when you are short with him when you are really angry with the movers who chipped a family heirloom plate. Just explain the situation as soon as you calm down. Children are very understanding.

Coping with Divorce

Half of today's young children are part of families that have undergone a divorce. It is not at all unusual to hear two four-year-olds discussing with which parent they will be spending the weekend. Divorce is a common occurrence in the lives of so many young children and so are the accompanying problems.

In many families, divorce is the culmination of months, perhaps years, of stress in the home. Children have overheard conversations they only partially understood and listened to fighting parents while no one explained to them the cause of the quarrel. It is no wonder that they are anxious and confused.

Even if the child of divorce was not subjected to these long-term strains at home, he is left with two reasons to feel stressed—guilt and separation.

Guilt

It is important to understand how a young child's mind works in order to see how he can feel responsible for a situation where, in our adult perceptions, he shares no blame. First, it is important to recognize that a child does not think like an adult—his lack of experience with how the world works does not allow him that maturity. A young child is very egocentric—he often sees things from his own point of view. Thus, he may think that when anything happens, he is the cause. If Mom gets a new job and there is a celebration at home, the young child feels that somehow he is the cause of her happiness; if someone in the family dies, he can feel that somehow he is to blame. In the same way, if his parents quarrel or divorce, a young child may feel responsible.

The young child is very empathetic—that is, he is sensitive to the feelings of others. He will frequently pick up on the feelings of hurt, betrayal, guilt, and anger that result no matter how "amicable" a divorce or separation may appear to his parents. Unfortunately, the child may be confused and not understand the cause of these feelings because he is not yet intellectually able to put himself in the position of those feeling the pain.

It is the job of parents and caring adults to help the child who is part of a divorce to know that he does not have magical power over all events—that he did not cause Mommy and Daddy to quarrel or Daddy to move out of the house. This may seem farfetched or silly to the adults involved, but this is really the way children often see the world until they are more mature. It is vitally important for the adults in the life of a young child to take responsibility for their behavior and their feelings, taking into account the child.

Parents involved in a divorce may feel anxious, depressed, and short tempered. These are natural reactions, but at the same time, they have to help their child learn that he is not responsible for the angry feelings.

Separation

Separation is an issue that we all face over and over in our lives. Some people have difficulty saying goodbye even as adults. Children can have an especially hard time leaving and being left–the degree depends on their age and personality. When your child was an infant, he was not bothered by your leaving him as long as someone was providing his basic needs. When he was about nine months old, your disappearance probably left him panic-stricken and enraged, at least for a few minutes. At 15 months, he really felt a sense of loss when you left him. The younger your child is, the more dependent he is on your care so the more anxious he gets when you go away. He is confused by time concepts. As he gets older, he begins to understand that when you leave you will return. A child of three is comforted by memories of you and knowing what you are doing while you are away. Even a five-year-old needs to know exactly where you are going and when you will return.

When one parent leaves the home, a young child experiences severe separation fears and pain. Often, the parent who stays at home is also suffering from the separation from his or her spouse. It is important for this parent and the other adults in his life not to deny the child's pain, but to discuss his feelings with him and to be sympathetic to unusual behavior. It is not unusual for a child involved in a divorce not to want to separate from his parent when he gets to school for fear of losing the remaining parent. He needs time to be sad, to be angry, and to cope with the separation.

But, a child of divorce **can** adjust to the situation. He needs constant support from the adults who care about him. If you are a parent in a divorce situation–or a friend or relative of a needy child–you can help. Here are some suggestions from Dr. Margery A. Kranyik.

▶ Be a good listener. Encourage your child to talk but do not appear to be prying. Let him know that you accept his feelings no matter what they are and that you are there for him whenever he needs you. Remember that hugs often work as well as words.

▶ You need to give your child a well-structured environment with regular routines and a lot of guidance from caring adults. More than ever, he needs to know his limits.

▶ Give your child some responsibilities to let him know that you still have expectations of him and that you trust him to do a good job.

▶ Help your child develop positive social relationships. Although children may need to be alone with their stress at times, they also need the support of friends. Try to seek out other children with divorced parents who can show your child that he is not alone with his problem.

▶ Work with your child's teachers to set up a support network for him. Tell them what is going on at home, and let them discuss how the child is acting in school. Don't hesitate to seek other professional help.

▶ Keep reminding your child how much both his parents care for him.

Visitations

It is very important that a child in a divorce maintain a feeling of love and respect for both of his parents. This will help his self-image and his ability to cope with the situation. Parents should encourage their child to draw pictures for both of them and send cards to the other parent when they are staying with one. If distance is not too great a problem, both parents should cooperate to see that visits are frequent and well-structured.

It is not unusual to find a child that spends Sunday afternoon with Dad, the summer with Mom, or every other weekend night in a different bed. Whether in the neighborhood or across the state, preparing a child for this kind of travel takes thought and planning. Here are some ideas to help make the transition from "home" to "home" easier.

▶ Set up a regular visiting schedule. Routines help everyone involved feel more secure. Show your child on a calendar when visits will occur and how long they will last.

▶ When your child is to be picked up from school by his other parent, make sure to let him know in advance, even if you have to telephone him at school. The shock of seeing someone he doesn't expect can ruin an otherwise pleasant reunion.

▶ Remind your child about 10 minutes before it's time to leave. *"Soon, Dad will be here to pick you up."* or *"In 10 minutes, we will be leaving to go to Mom's house."* If you tell him way ahead of time, you will only be building up anticipation and often anxieties.

▶ Allow favorite toys and "security blankets" to travel with your child. Let him help to pack his suitcase. He may have special clothes that he wants to wear for Dad or a new book he wants to share with Mom.

▶ Plan your time so that your child travels when he is well rested and not hungry. If he's going on a long car trip, take along a soft pillow and snacks.

▶ Be sensitive to the difficulty of the transition for your child. Tell him you understand if he is cranky or withdrawn, *"It's very hard to say hello to Daddy and goodbye to Mommy at the same time."*

▶ If you are the noncustodial parent, keep some familiar toys and "warm cuddlies" at your house to help your child feel as though he belongs there. Be sure to have one place—a room, a corner, or even a drawer—of his own.

▶ If your child makes angry comments occasionally, try not to take them personally. It's not uncommon for children to express their frustration at the situation through statements like, *"I wish I lived with Mommy,"* or *"This is yucky; I want to go home."* Have patience and try to help your child reflect on his feelings. *"Maybe you're angry that you can't be with both Mommy and Dad at the same time; I understand that you're sad when Daddy has to leave you, but we both love you and you will see him again on Saturday."*

By planning transitions and visits carefully and with your child's comfort and security foremost in your mind, you can help him maintain positive relationships with both of his parents.

Illness

Young children get sick. Especially when he starts school, your child will be exposed to all types of childhood diseases for the first time. He will be exposed to friends with runny noses and playmates who are "just getting over" one disease or another. If you follow the advice of your pediatrician about vitamins and general health care, then all you can do is to be aware of the signs that your child is coming down with something, keep him quiet and comfortable while he is ill, and be sure to take care of yourself a little--nursing is tiring and tedious.

TOGETHER

Make a Bird Feeder and place it outside a window where your child can see it from his bed.

How do you know if your child is ill? The first sign that something is wrong is often a change in your child's behavior. Although this change could be caused by stress as I have discussed or perhaps by problems at school, it may be, in fact, that your child is getting sick. You should be on the alert for additional signs of illness. These can include some of the following: dry mouth, unusually pale complexion, crankiness, shorter attention span, poor bladder control, and/or a dazed, glassy-eyed look.

When your child displays some of these symptoms, he may also revert to some seemingly babyish behavior. When he feels uncomfortable changes in his body over which he has no control, it is very normal for a child to need an extra dose of parental warmth and security. If he becomes clingy or whiny and wants to sit on your lap more than usual, he needs to be assured that he is going to be fine and that everyone feels sick sometimes.

Don't encourage your child to join in with other children or "rise above it" when he is not feeling well. He is in touch with the needs of his body better than anyone else. Don't make him feel worse because he doesn't have the energy to participate. If he has to stay in bed, make up a box or bag of "quiet activities" to keep him occupied. Include: paper, crayons, scissors, scotch tape, a magic slate, kaleidoscope, magnifying glass, stickers, paper clips, a magnet, pipe cleaners, and an old pack of playing cards.

If your child is going to have to stay in a hospital, encourage him to talk about his expectations and fears. Have him play hospital with his stuffed animals. Let him be the doctor or nurse with control over the make-believe situation.

Remember that you are your child's primary model when it comes to "patient behavior." If you want to help your child understand that illness is part of life and not to worry about it, you have to model that behavior when you are ill. Do you carry on and complain a lot? Do you call the doctor and then follow his advice? What is your attitude with your child--impatient, accepting, worried, annoyed, overwhelmed? Your child is a keen observer when you are sick. How you act will help him form his own patterns of behavior and attitudes towards doctors and illness. Even illness is a learning experience for your young child. He learns that there are times when he needs special help and that he can trust others to take care of him at those times.

BIRD FEEDER

YOU'LL NEED:

 large pine cone

cord

 spoon

 peanut butter

 suet

 bird seed

waxed paper

WHAT TO DO:

1. Tie cord to top petals of pine cone.

2. Spoon peanut butter and suet between pine cone petals.

3. Place bird seed on waxed paper.

4. Roll peanut butter pine cone in bird seed.

5. Hang feeder in tree near child's bedroom, if possible.

Encounters with Death

If death should enter your child's world—whether it is a relative, friend, or a pet—he needs your warmth and patience in order to deal with the experience in a healthy way. It is important for you to help him come to an understanding of what has happened and to work through the grief of separation. Your natural instinct may be to protect your child from the pain and sorrow, but avoiding the issue does more harm than good. Your child needs to talk about the loved one who has died, perhaps even to see him or her in death in order to process the experience, mourn, and finally let go. In this instance, a child's needs are much like an adult's.

Both during and after the experience, be open to all of your child's questions. Take them seriously, even if your child appears to be acting silly when he asks them—this may be due to nervousness or grief or both. Talk together about the person or pet's life—and death.

Your child might like to make a MEMORY BOOK. This book can include pictures by your child of special times shared with the deceased and favorite things like books, songs, games, and foods that they enjoyed together. Let your child choose a favorite photograph of himself and the deceased together for the cover. Making a book like this is usually more meaningful than the end result. Your child may wish to put it away. Respect his feelings.

Since young children have not developed a real sense of time yet, your child may become very concerned that you or he will die soon. After all, a deceased relative may have been very elderly, but that term has no meaning for him. You are old in comparison to him. It is better to show, rather than tell, him that the person or pet in question lived "a long, long time." Make a timeline with your child showing significant times in his life, yours, and perhaps his grandparents. Show him what a "long, long time" really looks like.

Read books together about the death of a loved one. The Tenth Good Thing About Barney by Judith Viorst and Nana Upstairs and Nana Downstairs by Tomie dePaola are classics on this subject. A good reference book for you is Should the Children Know? Encounters with Death in the Lives of Children by Marguerita Rudolph. Written by a former teacher, it deals with actual experiences of children and the deaths of playmates and classroom pets. It is a very sensitive and insightful book.

When dealing with the death of a pet, many children need the ritual of a little service and some kind of burial to help them separate from a beloved animal. Your child might want to compose a poem about his pet and then construct a little marker with natural materials like stones and wood scraps.

When you are mourning, share your grief with your child. For all of us, it helps to talk to someone and children are sympathetic listeners. The joy of loving and the pain of parting are both parts of real life—a life we want to help our children live to its fullest.

Siblings

Rivalry

When there is more than one child in the family, there are special stresses. How many brothers and sisters your child has, the order of birth in the family, and the relationship between family members may all be factors affecting how your child behaves. Being aware of how these factors operate assists you in helping your child develop self-esteem and social skills. The first group that your child belongs to is his family. Therefore, it is very important that he feel that he is a special member of this group. This will affect how he behaves in other group situations. Whether your child is the first-born, the middle, the baby, or an only child, often determines his attitudes and behavior.

Perhaps your child is the first-born child in the family. It is typical for the first-born to be a perfectionist. If his jacket is missing a button, he might refuse to wear it or if he makes a mistake in a drawing, he may tear up his paper. He is not usually very tolerant when things do not go as he expects them to. The first child may have a hard time adjusting to school initially because he is always first at home but it is hard to be "first" at school. The first child is usually a strong individual but he may need special help in learning to share, compromise, and do things as part of a group.

The second–or middle–child has a different set of circumstances and problems to deal with. While his first-born sibling is often responsible, hard-working, and cooperative, your second child may be stubborn or withdrawn, overly aggressive or shy–in other words, totally different from your first child. He may work so hard at school that he is a star or he may take the opposite tack and not live up to his potential. Being different may be the only way he knows to stand out and be special. Your second child does not want to be like his older brother or sister. He will go to great lengths to avoid the inevitable comparisons. You have to be very sensitive to your middle child and give special attention to his strengths–never comparing them to his sibling's. Pick up on his interests and plan special times around them.

The youngest child in the family has another difficult problem. If your preschooler is the "baby," he may have a hard time getting out of this role and becoming independent and self-confident. Often, other people in a family take pleasure in doing things for the youngest member. He doesn't get the chance to do for himself. That is why he will run crying to an adult when someone takes his toy–he doesn't have the experience or the confidence to handle the problem himself.

Another potentially serious problem for younger and youngest siblings arises when they try to be like their older sisters or brothers. Instead of rebelling as the second child often does, there may be a situation where a younger child feels that he has to do the same as his older siblings. You have to be very firm and patient with the younger child, constantly pointing out that he is just fine as he is. AND, you have to protect him from the teasing and ridicule when he tries to be grown up and falls on his face.

With all of these complicated feelings, it is no wonder that siblings don't always get along. They quarrel, argue, tattle on each other, hit--it takes many forms. Because you want your children to be friendly, cooperative, loving, and good to each other, you may forget that it is really all right for children to argue and fight sometimes, as long as no one gets hurt. Safety is always your first consideration. When there is danger, step in immediately.

Whenever you take sides, one child "wins" and the other automatically "loses" and no one really learns from the experience. And, unless you observed the whole situation, you really don't know all the facts. For example, your four-year-old son may come running to you with a torn drawing screaming because his younger sister ripped it. What you don't know is that he was waving it in front of her face and she thought it was a game to tear it. Don't get involved in discussions of who is "right." Tell your children that you believe in them and their ability to sort things out themselves.

If you feel that you need to get involved, help the children face each other and encourage each one to talk about what happened. Support them while they work out an answer together.

A New Baby

Sibling rivalry is a fact of life, but so are the warm, wonderful feelings that siblings have for each other and the special times they share. If your young child has no older sibling--or even if he does--you may be planning a new addition to the family. This will be a time of great joy for the whole family, but don't forget that it will also be a time of stress for the about-to-be older brother or sister. No matter how intrigued he is by the concept of a new baby, the reality will make him feel displaced and he will need your help and support to make adjustments.

TOGETHER

Make this Soft Baby with your child, "someone" for him to take care of, to cuddle, and sleep with, to take out frustrations and jealousies on.

Remember that even though the baby is adorable and seemingly helpless, your sturdy preschooler's feelings are much more fragile at his stage of development and he needs just as much--if not more--cuddling, hugging, and nurturing as the new arrival. Take the time during the pregnancy to talk to your child about what is going on. Show him pictures of when he was an infant. These photos of him being held and cared for will underscore the fact that he was, and is loved. If you are having a baby shower, make sure that he is included and that he receives gifts for being the big brother(sister). When the baby arrives, encourage your child to hand out pink or blue lollipops or pencils at school and to his friends.

Once the baby is born, spend time with your older child looking at photo albums and mementos of special times spent together. Look through this book and encourage your child to pick out his favorite activities. Tell him that he and his new sibling can do these projects TOGETHER in a few years. That will be a really SPECIAL TIME for you!

SOFT BABY

YOU'LL NEED:

1 stretch suit-zippered type is best

child's hat or cap

polyester stuffing

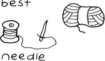

scissors

yarn (use child's hair color)

needle and thread

embroidery thread (use child's eye color)

OR

old nylon stocking or polyester fabric

WHAT TO DO:

1. Sew arms of stretch suit closed. Sew up the snaps or zip up zipper. Stuff with polyester stuffing.

2. Cut out an 8" circle from stocking or fabric. Sew and gather edges to make a small bag-like shape. Stuff with polyester stuffing.

3. Use needle and thread to sew a soft sculpture face. Use embroidery thread to make eyes.

4. Sew on loops of yarn for hair.

5. Attach head securely to body with needle and thread.

6. Sew on hat or cap to head.